D1603319

THE MISSION OF THE PROPHETS

ADRIENNE VON SPEYR

THE MISSION
OF THE
PROPHETS

FOREWORD BY HANS URS VON BALTHASAR

TRANSLATED BY DR. DAVID KIPP

IGNATIUS PRESS   SAN FRANCISCO

Title of the German original:
Die Sendung der Propheten
© 1953 Johannes Verlag, Einsiedeln
Published with ecclesiastical approval

Cover art: *Moses on Mt. Sinai*
S. Vitale, Ravenna, Italy
Scala/Art Resource, New York

Cover design by Roxanne Mei Lum

© 1996 Ignatius Press, San Francisco
All rights reserved
ISBN 0-89870-593-2
Library of Congress catalogue number 96-83644
Printed in the United States of America ∞

CONTENTS

FOREWORD

This little book is the introduction to—or first part
of—a comprehensive work on the missions of the
New Covenant that will appear later and be based
essentially on the same methodological presupposi-
tions: consideration and contemplation, in prayer, of
the supernatural reality concealed in the Word of God,
combined with an impartial openness, an attitude of
service extending almost to self-forgetfulness, so that
only what is objective in revelation might show itself.

Thematically central here is the concept of mission,
which plays an all-governing part in both the Old and
the New Testament. Mission is not (as is often wrongly
assumed) the simple resultant of two components: a
universal grace that is offered to everyone in the same
way and the different historical, psychological, and
biographical factors that condition any individual recipient of that grace. Rather, mission is that particular
and unique form of grace which God intends, and
holds ready, for each recipient of mission and which,
while certainly existing in a relationship of mysterious,
never-definable harmony with the individual's natural
conditions, can still rule sovereignly over those conditions, requiring that they be wholly subordinated and
placed at its disposal. This is supremely true of those
individual choices and missions that, under the Old

Covenant, are bearers of the process of revelation itself or that, under the New Covenant, subserve the ever-renewed explication and vitalization of revelation as something enduringly present and active in the Mystical Body of Jesus Christ. These missions were, from the very beginning, both personal and historical: different and new in every case, always surprising, never to be calculated or deduced in advance; and it is precisely as such that they are the authentic revelation of ever-flowing grace, whose essential historicality cannot be exhaustively captured in any general precepts. From the standpoint of man, only one thing is possible: to place oneself wholly at the disposal of unforeseeable grace; to avoid wanting to determine anything, to anticipate anything. Nature is, and remains, clay in the hands of God, and no one but God knows just which forms he will bring forth out of you or me.

Inquiry into the missions of the Old Covenant also implies coming to know, in and through God's revelation, both God himself and his inner being; listening to his Word, which is essentially a Word having its effects in man; and observing man and his way of behaving under God's formative hand. It is, therefore, an altogether central vantage point that Adrienne von Speyr adopts here. From that position, she meditates upon a number of the greatest figures in the Old Testament. Her main concern is with these figures themselves, their inner decisions, their prayers, their tasks, their fulfillment of the roles that God has assigned to them—as opposed to the external succession of events and how that succession was decisively influenced by them (something that, as such, can be looked up in any account of biblical history). From time to time, the reader of the present book will probably feel urged to consult his Bible in order to make comparisons. Well may he do so, for it is only through immersion in the Word of revelation itself (which is how the authoress' own expositions were engendered) that the most profound meanings behind the images of mission can become accessible. For purposes of reference, the table of contents includes a listing of the relevant biblical texts.

Today, the concept of Christian mission has been grasped in essence by many Christians. They have understood that grace always conceals within itself a task, that chosenness always demands a commitment to the unchosen. But if we are to do justice to our mission, we must look to the saints of revelation and of the Church—not in order to copy them slavishly, which would be impossible anyway, but to learn from them how man needs to subordinate himself, in unperturbed humility, to the directives of God. There are those who speak of mission today when what they really mean is some self-conceived program. But what reveals itself in mission, as nowhere else, is the majesty and absolute sovereignty of God, who chooses whom he wishes, in order to send him where he wishes, with that mission which he forms and infuses into the words and life of his messenger.

HANS URS VON BALTHASAR
May 1953

ABRAHAM

This is a threefold mission. It begins with Abraham's having the initially unprovable certainty—in his faith and in his prayer, in his everyday attitude, and at times when he is specifically speaking with God—that he has a mission. This mission appears to him as an imperceptible sort of chosenness. He knows that he has to behave as a marked man, that God expects something of him and will also give him something, that he must be especially faithful and devout and just. This quiet preassurance remains wholly in the depths of his soul; it corresponds, at this first stage, to no vision of any external task, no pathway, and no definite experience. It is like being quite gently shaken—it is barely perceivable yet still occasions a corresponding awareness. He must live as a bearer of mission, which means being constantly heedful of himself in order for God's intentions to become clear through him.

There is a second dimension to this mission, one characterized more by a kind of persistence. Abraham must remain subject for a time to what he has experienced so as to allow it to grow fuller. And when he is eventually asked to sacrifice his son, he suddenly realizes: he is the father of the promise on the human plane. He himself is not the object; God wishes, through him, to effect something greater. What is important is not his own person but that which God has implanted in him. This is the dimension that includes his family, the generations descending from him, the whole people, as symbolized by his son, Isaac. He cannot imagine what God intends; he has simply to persist in this course of things. To go on expanding the foundation of his faith, allowing his prayer to deepen. Behaving at all times as if he were a kind of mission-bearer from God.

The third dimension is the confirmation of his mission. That mission belongs no longer to him but to the whole of the Old Covenant—in fact, to the whole world. He is merely the earthly basis, the worldly mirror image, for the activity of the Father in heaven. The Father is the bearer of the promises; the Father is the one who actually sacrifices his Son; the Father is also obedient in relation to the mission of the Son, who is embodied in Isaac, even though the latter gains no clear experience of this. But for Abraham, too, this is no longer something personally experienced. He recedes into the background; Isaac recedes into the background; their actions recede into the background. Everything is merely a sign. A symbol, about which the actors understand little, yet which is rewarded and proves correct. But a sign that points down through the ages, all the way to the end of time. In Abraham is Christ, is the New Covenant. The two look toward each other like mirror images in implicit supplementation; the one is prefiguration, the other fulfillment.

Three missions in one. A small, unambitious, occasionally almost hopeless obedience, which yet constitutes the whole joy, the whole pride, of the race and brings with it the highest of rewards, inasmuch as the triune God sees fit to make the history of Abraham the means for proclaiming the prehistory of the Incarnation of God.

ISAAC

Isaac's mission lies between that of Abraham and that of Christ. His place is established already on the lap of Abraham; in his submission to whatever is to happen to him, to his lot as an intended sacrifice, he illustrates the obedience of his father; indeed, even before his first appearance, from the time of his birth onward, he illustrates the special position of Abraham. But this function is altogether oriented toward suggesting the promise of Christ; and thus it corresponds in a sense to the first dimension of the mission of Abraham. In those contexts, however, where the son Isaac is intended to represent the Son, Jesus, the person of Abraham recedes into the background and Isaac's relationship with his father alludes directly to the heavenly Father. It is before him that he must exemplify how a man lives in the time of promise, corresponding to how the Son of God will live in that of fulfillment. The Son will state everlastingly that he has come in order to glorify the Father and to accomplish his will. To this corresponds the fact that Isaac is continually blessed for his father's sake, that the blessings accorded him point back toward the father and are intended for him. So, too, the Redeemer constantly points back toward the Creator. What we have here, then, is a mission within the mission of Abraham as well as one that prefigures the mission of the Son. Isaac's entire faith, his entire piety, his assumption of the promise and his life within that promise: all this is a prototype of the Son and his acceptance of the fulfillment and his fulfillment of the fulfillment. And just as Isaac's conception within the barren Sarah is shrouded in mystery, so the Incarnation of the Son in a virgin—heralded by the birth of the Baptist from the barren Elizabeth—will point back to mysteries that are of the Father. In matters concerning the promise, the Creator breaks through those laws that he has decreed for his creation; he will also break them in the context of the fulfillment, but inasmuch as this second breaking points back to an earlier prototype—indeed, inasmuch as the choosing of the Virgin as mother points even farther back to the Creator's original intentions in paradise—any appearance of arbitrariness in the breaking is effectively precluded: it demonstrates the higher lawfulness inherent in the actions of the Creator. The new miracle is reinforced by the experience of the old.

On the other hand, the sacrifice of Isaac is not ultimately carried out, whereas Jesus permits his own to be carried through to the end. His sacrificial death is followed by his Resurrection. The sacrifice of Isaac is followed by the old mode of life. Whereas the sacrifice of the Cross points ahead to the coming new age, the sacrifice of Isaac points to the established old age. One refers forward, the other backward. Insofar as the two sacrifices are related to each other, the two ages reach out to each other.

Isaac's mission is not, of course, one of understanding, of surpassing, of new teaching. It is one contained within that of Abraham, whose meaning lies in allowing oneself to be revealed, emptied, divested: a kenosis oriented toward the New Covenant that is understandable only in relation to the New Covenant. It is the assumption of the promise at the time of its devolving upon Abraham. The words that are spoken, the things that are done, provide only a substructure for what happens with the Son, who refers back to them: "It is written!" Only after the mysteries surrounding the Son are disclosed, to the extent willed by the Father, so that the force of revelation can be comprehended, does a light fall upon what was implicit in Isaac while deriving from Abraham, just as Christ will derive his mystery from the Father. And the human race is included in the chain that links Abraham to the Virgin Mary: it is preredeemed at the time of promise and redeemed at the time of fulfillment—indeed, redeemed back through all time by the Cross, because the time of promise took the course that God had conceived for it, because God had bestowed his favor and his pity upon Abraham and because Abraham, comprehending yet still not comprehending, accepted from the hands of the Father the obedience that the Father would bestow anew upon his Son.

JACOB

From the beginning of time the Spirit was there, within the triune God, ready to be sent forth, to act as a mediator for the purpose of educating man in the knowledge of God. Were it not for sin, the Son would not have been sent, the mission of the Spirit would not have become apparent at the sensory level; it would have operated in a way reminiscent of the interchange of love within the tripersonal life of the Divinity. Then men would not only have sensed and experienced the expatiations of God in paradise but would have participated, through the Holy Spirit, in the intradivine conversation. When men fall into sin, a new plan of God's is revealed, which includes the setting out of new decrees and positions for men regarding the Father's righteousness and his love, the Son's love and his righteousness, and the breath of the Spirit in his righteousness and his love of Father and Son. Correspondingly, types of mission are differentiated and allocations are made. The Spirit separates out his individual gifts, and the faithful to whom they are apportioned must learn to distinguish not only between the Spirit of God and the evil spirit but also among the individual gifts of the divine Spirit. From this point on, there exists something like a disputation of man with God that is carried out under the offices of the

Spirit. And to this corresponds a disputation of God with man. There are now individual segments to the history of redemption, comparatively different "share certificates" in the assets of heaven. And there is a kind of hierarchy among missions, all having the one common aspect of being oriented toward the Son. Under the Old Covenant, they point ahead to the Son; under the New Covenant, they originate from the Son and point back again to him. And the missions are quite diverse.

In Jacob, something of this diversity becomes visible, something of the profuseness of the varied forms that God has at his disposal. Jacob participates in the most significant part of what distinguishes and defines the might of heaven, the supernatural as opposed to the natural. He does not lose his own place on earth but must, from that standpoint, apprehend and experience whatever of the supernatural God mediates and learn to submit himself to that. In everything that befalls him, he must, above all, be obedient. He has a mission of obedience. In his dream he must behold what God shows to him. In his struggle with the angel he must undergo what it means to wrestle with the presence of God. In his obtaining Isaac's blessing he must learn to understand the predominance of divine over human truth. His lie is not a personal one; what appears to be deception is not humanly conditioned but something willed by God, so that God's mightiness and powers of intervention, and his incomprehensible truth, might become known anew, in all their unpredictability, through Jacob. Even if Jacob could not state it expressly, he goes through an experience of obedience transcending the spheres of tradition, life, belief, and understanding. If God were subsequently to let him fall, Jacob would perhaps no longer comprehend how he could have deceived his blind father, usurped the right of primogeniture from his brother, struggled against God, and done so many things that exceeded the scope of his human responsibility. But God holds him, just as he holds all those he sends: up above understanding, so that new understanding might be created, new perspectives thrown open, new horizons brought into view.

Jacob is, to be sure, linked firmly into the Old Testament chain of tradition, between his fathers and his sons, just as his own father was placed between father and son, in the inexorableness of a chain that is formed before it is recognized, one in which there is neither a "being too late" nor a "still having time", because it extends down into time from eternity, unbreakably forged, yet also full of promise, so that it can, as a whole, be accepted and borne. Jacob takes over that which he must receive in order to pass it on in a form that he himself may not define, since it has been predetermined from time immemorial. He is a son and a grandson, a descendant. But he is also a founder and an initiator. Thus he stands at the middle yet connects the extremes. He is compliant yet self-willed, and his unjustness is enclosed within the justness of God to which it belongs: so that he might serve to exemplify how God repeatedly finds and treads new pathways, how his possibilities are inexhaustible, how man is but a plaything in his hands when it comes to achieving his ends: because the first man sinned, and from then on no man any longer participates in the shaping of his own destiny. And in everything that befalls Jacob, he experiences not himself but the way of God. Even when he proves inadequate and fails to recognize the magnitude of his mission, or even lacks any awareness that he has been sent, he is nevertheless always one summoned, who follows after and comes before.

JOSEPH

From the human viewpoint, this is a mission centered on the notion of the "nevertheless"; from the divine viewpoint, it is one subserving the greater glory of God who confers it. To be sure, there is perhaps less talk of God in it than in the missions that preceded it and more reference instead, again and again, to the behavior of Joseph—of his becoming and remaining conscious of his task, which dwells with him in such a way that he himself watches over it. The mission is entrusted to him. He knows this from the very start. He senses it already as a child, and in the years of his youth he becomes fully conscious of it. When he finds himself living through strange events, when his brothers attempt to bring about his downfall together with that of the mission that sets him apart, then not only does God act to defend him, but he defends himself. He knows that he must answer personally, before God, for that which has been entrusted to him. Although he no doubt lives a life of prayer, it is primarily a life of purity, guardianship, and obedience. In some of its aspects, it can hardly be compared with others, because the things that happen externally are very remarkable, and it is only on the basis of the concrete responses to external events that a correct conception of an inner life can emerge. He has dreams. He interprets dreams.

One could just as well use the term "visions". For what he sees is inspired by God, and the responses that he knows to make are responses of prayer, responses in God. Thus he lives in intuitive closeness with the world of God, the supernatural world, to which neither his brothers nor the rest of those around him have any access. If a dream comes to the king, it is like catching hold of a fragment of a mission; he is permitted a quick look into the supernatural, but he is no saint; he does not know what purpose it serves; he is incapable of interpreting it, nor does God interpret it for him; rather, God allows—because it was his will from the very beginning—Joseph to provide the interpretation, to know the answer, to articulate it, on God's behalf, in its complete truth.

Joseph is available for every sort of service. He lets himself be shown the dreams about the sun, moon, and stars and about the sheaves, and he comprehends their meaning. He also comprehends the envy of his brothers. But danger is an inherent part of his undertakings. He knows, when fleeing from Potiphar's wife, that this act of purity will be dangerous for him. Yet he can distinguish very well between a man and his commission. What is dangerous for the man can be of no concern to the commissioned. What seems unworkable when assessed in human terms must be achievable in the context of the mission. His mission is one of "nevertheless"; it must succeed, it must be struggled with and kept intact to the very end. And when he finally acquires an honored position, when his voice becomes a weighty one and his fame spreads throughout the lands, then he remains aware that this fame pertains to his mission, which is contained in God, that everything is really God's fame. He knows how to distinguish between what is his and what is God's. He does not become an unfaithful custodian who regards the goods entrusted to him as his own possessions. He watches over what he has because it is on loan from God. And when, in all the luster of his high standing, he meets up again with his father and brothers, he remains as unaffected as he was in the beginning, always intent on using his position to serve the greater glory of God. Not only personally, but also through the way that others see his position. He knows himself to be a mediator, but one who has been sent. And he knows exactly what sort of balance he must maintain in his life between acquiescence and contemplation and action, because his stance before God is always such as to enable the contours of the divine paths that God has designated specifically for him to become clear to him. He does not stray beyond those paths. Even when he is in alien territory and feels abandoned and lonely because (despite his earlier dream) his view into what lies ahead, of future reunion, is not always distinct, he still never loses the certainty that he must preserve the heritage of his fathers and hand it on to his sons. All his wanderings, the deed of his brothers, his imprisonments and rejections—nothing can stand in the way of what God wills. In and through everything the mission goes forward.

MOSES

This whole mission has a likeness to creation. God creates it and moves ahead with it from one day of creation to the next, regardless of all obstacles, regardless of whatever has been, in order to construct what must come to be. Just as when, in the beginning, God creates heaven and earth, separates the waters from dry land, populates the earth, and brings forth the sun and moon, all with hardly any connection being initially evident between the works of the individual days, so, too, the mission of Moses seems to consist of disconnected parts that begin to take on a comprehensive aspect and to reveal the unity both of the mission and of God's blessing and chastising interventions only with the passing of time and especially in the light of the New Covenant.

The circumstances following his birth, his recovery from the river, his saving flight into exile are like exclamation points meant to attract attention, not just then but also today. The uniqueness of the mission is constituted in solitude, in withdrawal. Then there ensues a long development: a struggling, a need for sustained self-assertion, a not wanting to continue, a sudden sense of authority, and yet again a weakness—those means that nature devises in order to fend off the supernatural, those to which the individual resorts in fear so as to avoid the issue, to lead a life of his own, to be allowed to submerge himself in the masses, to forget that he is an individual.

Then suddenly there is the power that God confers on him, as if it were his own, and the performance of miracles, as if they were his own. It is part of his task to perform them in that manner until he has progressed sufficiently and knows God well enough to begin performing them only in God's name, because he is no longer allowed to construct intermediary elements, to interpose himself, but must be nothing more than an instrument in God's hands, even in circumstances where his own nature and reason would point him in other directions. And the many signs that he must actualize, pre-Christian signs, are there so that, later on, the Son and his followers can refer to them for the purpose of evidencing the Son's eternal nature, of showing how grace is constituted, of enabling conceptions about eternal time to be clarified. Moses is the servant of God; he does what he is bidden to do, alternatively experiencing a withdrawal of understanding and a need for having to understand, in a sequential order whose law no man is capable of penetrating yet which implicitly contains the dawnings of grace, the beginning of obedience, indeed, the imitation of Christ. But in such a way that Moses must apprehend God's word like a blind man who hears something without being able to see any form. And again and again comes the grace that he mediates to the people, which is closely tied to his serving as intermediary yet is quite beyond his capacity to control. And, finally, the grace of the water from the rock, when he is slow to unlock the spring and is subsequently punished for it out of grace. He will not be allowed to enter the Promised Land but is to lead the people to it. And again, together with that punishment and the awareness of his guilt and failing, he is a symbol of the coming missions of the Christian age, whose bearers must learn to forego the fruits so that they might not merely praise obedience blindly but adhere to it as well. That Moses is denied entry into the Promised Land is grace; grace arising out of punishment, grace for those still to come, who can draw support from it when accepting their mission blindly from the hands of God. And the things he experiences at the personal level—the honors, the grumblings of the people, his encounters in friendship with God, his hesitation, his doubts about the rightness of what God demands—all manifest the play of God's hand with the human soul, which, for its part, repeatedly bristles and brusquely demurs. But through all the rifts and fissures there remains the constancy of the supernatural. And the greatness of God.

To the same extent that this whole mission is self-contained and directed toward the salvation of the people, it is simultaneously a mission of perspectives, of openings, of forces at play; for the mission is one of grace, repeatedly pointing toward God as the Ever-greater, but also toward God the Son, to the meaning of suffering, to the Cross in general, and, via the Cross, repeatedly to the Father. Via the Cross, inasmuch as the mission-bearing man is himself given a life of the Cross that takes on meaning solely in and through grace. Moses, considered solely as himself, would be almost nothing, perhaps a kind of adventurer whose life is filled with remarkable events. But the order in which those events occur is repeatedly indicative of the guiding force of grace, of the essence of grace. Moses is tossed to and fro so as to attest, in every sort of situation, to the fact that grace is omnipresent. He is like a textbook example, transferred to the world, of the omnipresence of divine grace, both in himself and absolutely; but also for the people, and ultimately for the Son and his followers, who, in referring to him, are able to point, simultaneously, back through the ages and into the future.

AARON

His is a mission of contradiction. It occupies a position midway between God and the mission of Moses; again, it is midway between office and nonoffice; and yet again midway between the multitude and the individual. The zigzag course of this mission is well suited to clarifying intuitively these three midway positions and their relative planes, to allowing the form of God's interaction with man, with the people of the covenant, to become manifest—with the covenant appearing as the pre-Church, the office as a forerunner of ecclesiastical office, and the midway position between God and Moses as a preform of the "intercession of saints", of the loving Church. To be sure, the New Covenant is still quite far away. But God makes use of Aaron for the purpose of exhibiting grace and nongrace: in a light that will reveal its full luster only after the Incarnation of the Son yet still suffices, in its early dimness, to reveal the vastnesses of God and the vastnesses into which he has placed man.

Since Moses does not want to accept the mission that was intended for him, God brings in Aaron, and Aaron has to want it. He has to want it out of not wanting it; he has to develop out of his brother's No, which God wants to make into a Yes. Hence, his mission is, in its very origins, internally contradictory: it is as if someone would have to become holy out of another's refusal to be holy. That this can, in fact, be done is a sign of the all-surpassing power of God. God places Aaron right in the midst of Moses' No, and it is Aaron's task to wrest that No from Moses and see that it ultimately becomes a Yes. The companionship of Aaron is intended to help strengthen Moses. Moses, in turn, represents the position of God for Aaron. In relation to Aaron, Moses behaves as the holy one, because he possesses the word. Were it really possible to classify missions as greater and lesser, Aaron would have to rank far below Moses. Aaron is a man of the people. He represents the people, lets himself be influenced by the people, and experiences in his soul the indecisiveness that, from then onward, no longer affects Moses. Out of Moses' unfaithfulness has come the faithfulness of Aaron; yet in that very faithfulness dwells an unfaithfulness, through which Moses can, in turn, be faithful.

In Moses, God creates an office, and indeed the supreme office, to which Aaron, even as high priest, is subordinate. Also, Aaron draws a distinction between office and personality, allowing himself to be critical in contexts where he should really be only obedient. He is punished so that he might become more perceptive. But he lacks the holiness required for seeing punishment as grace; before every punishment, he trembles and pleads for remission. When he is punished nonetheless, this lends an increased depth to his mission: a momentary new obedience is thereby generated, yet he is incapable of keeping pace with that obedience and with the breadth of his mission. Time and again, he is mercilessly flung back into the No of Moses, which was there at the start of both these missions; he must take it upon himself as his own No, so that Moses might then say Yes. Thus he cannot be left alone. When Moses disappears for a time, the presence of God becomes remote for Aaron. God has, in effect, caused a sword to be suspended above him by embodying himself, for him, in Moses. But Aaron does not sense his distancing from God; he simply drifts away. Basically, he would need to be held fast continually by some small, perceptible, and close bond.

Then again, he does what he is given to do with touching compliance; he is a man of prayer and humility. But he cannot tolerate the solitude of the desert. He cannot ascend the mountain alone, cannot be left behind alone, cannot be alone without some evident presence. To him, absence means the No, weakness, a falling away. He also stands midway between the masses and God; when God becomes invisible to him, the masses acquire guiding force over him; he lets himself be swayed one way, then another, in the belief that he is rescuing something. But he rescues only his own personality, viewed at the fully human level rather than grasped as being in office or in God. And yet he is a skilled speaker; when God's word is imparted to him, he can communicate it truly and effectively. His is a mission with a supporting prop. In this prop, which has manifest form in Moses and collapses when Moses is not there, God provides an example of grace. He demonstrates how his presence is constantly required so that the mission-bearer might not fall but can accomplish his work while dwelling in grace. Aaron has to experience, in the good as well as the bad sense, what it means to allow things to happen. If Moses is present, what he allows to happen is what God wishes. If Moses is absent, what he allows to happen is whatever nonobedience imposes on him. Aaron does not have the strength to maintain a position of uninterrupted affirmation because he remains trapped within the No of Moses. It is a mission of a kind that would no longer be possible under the New Covenant. When a holy man interacts with God under the New Covenant, there is no course open but that of faithfulness; should he lapse from that, he forfeits irrevocably the badge of his mission. It is part of God's justice under the Old Covenant that he continually revives Aaron, always allows him to make a new start, because God himself has generated him out of the No. And the vacillations between the No and the Yes, between willing and not willing, being and not being, are ultimately allusions to Adam: after the fall, before the fall, after the fall again, and before the fall again—as if in an everlasting cancellation of temporality, which will be ordered anew by God after Christ, so that for Aaron, too, everything negative will become part of an antecedent past, while everything affirmative will be strung together to form an unbroken chain in which he can appear before God as bearer of his office.

JOSHUA

Joshua's mission consists first of all in an attitude of openness toward God so that, through a process of interplay between nature and the supernatural, the moderately talented man can appear as zealous and constantly reinspired by faith. He finds his master in Moses. For him, Moses has a significance like that of a patron saint, or a favorite saint, for a Catholic. Through the medium of Moses, his bond with God is constantly strengthened; by striving, in a wholly personal way, to emulate Moses, he gradually acquires the manner of thinking, and indeed the characteristic nature, of a son. And Moses, in turn, sees him as his pupil and successor. Initially, this succession need not be at all obvious, yet everything points toward its coming about. Moses delegates certain tasks to Joshua, in accordance with his abilities, that he has to accomplish in place of, or together with, the master—as if Moses were the director and Joshua the actor who always has his role assigned to him or is even told how to speak, gesture, or perform in general. Up to a certain point, he is permitted to accompany Moses in his encounters with God.

One might be inclined to draw conclusions from this about certain levels of contemplation: Joshua accompanies Moses up to a certain level, but the central experience of the encounter with God is reserved for the greater of the two. However, it is perhaps less a matter of levels than one of shared awareness. Of being assimilated to the paramount position. Joshua is allowed to go along, too, so that he might become, as such, a mission-bearer before God; might accompany the prophet with his prayers while Moses is speaking with God and being instructed by him; and might regard his nonparticipation not as a slight, but in a positive sense: as the accompanying role that is suited to him and has been so arranged by God and Moses. An awareness, then, of the contemplation, perhaps even an enabling of that contemplation, because in this way the prophet knows that he is not alone and forsaken but is accompanied, up to whichever point God has determined, by his servant. Thus the prayer of Moses encompasses an apparently necessary element of contemplation, by Joshua, of his contemplation—something smaller, farther removed, that is nevertheless suited to broadening Joshua's spirit, to giving him the capacity for later tasks, to extending his limits (even if imperceptibly to him) so that Moses can implant still more.

The existence of such limits becomes clear in his cavilling response to the spiritually gifted. Joshua does not possess the discernment of spirits; he does not grasp the essence of the prophetic. He sees it concentrated in his master, also perhaps as having been thus concentrated by the will of God, and sees how it manifests itself in the master's directives; but he does not recognize the Spirit in detachment from Moses, does not know him as freely soaring, self-activating, as the one who blows where he will; he cannot distinguish what is sanctioned by God from what is pursued by men and may be deeply imbued with human desires. This incident is well suited to exposing what is limited, what is merely imitative, in Joshua and, hence, at the same time, to illumining the sacramental, the conferment of the office of high priest, the grace of the laying on of hands—which turns a man of limited capabilities into a truly capable one, a chosen individual whose talent seems inadequate into one wholly possessed by grace. The relationship between the stages of precommission and postcommission is clearly illustrated by the case of Joshua: in his precommission phase, he may be regarded as the bondsman of the prophet, up to that moment when the "sacrament" unlocks him, transforms his obedience into a new one, and sets him beyond the limitedness of his aptitude. The change is not due, as one might think, to progress over time, to learning from experience, to the fruits of being instructed. It is due entirely to the office, that office which, if properly understood, expands the mission toward the illimitable, toward whatever is willed by God. And when, from that point on, Joshua, in the office that he has taken over from Moses, leads the people, he no longer falls short of the master; he accepts the task from Moses' hands in order to see that it is carried out as would have been proper in complete obedience to the mission of Moses. The successor proves worthy of his master. The little stream that had been running for some time alongside the great river now flows into that river and becomes a powerful torrent. This force was imparted to the office by God.

BALAAM

This is a mission of the sort that no longer is possible under the New Covenant. In the New Covenant, the Son carried every sin to the Cross, after which missions can no longer be interrupted with impunity by grave sins on the part of those involved. There are many missions that can be rightly pursued for part of their way but then go astray, and this wrong turn destroys the good that preceded it. With Balaam it is different; his case serves to illustrate what was possible under the Old Covenant.

First there is the presence of natural reason, which permits even heathens to have knowledge of Yahweh, so that, from their pagan standpoint, they can know things correctly about God and can fear him. Balaam knows God not just in theory, like an idea, but knows him in practice, in his power and actuality. This is then supplemented by the appearance of God: the Spirit who draws near to him so that he recognizes him, hears his voice, and obeys his command. One cannot speak of genuine faith here, because the knowing, listening, and acting are not integrated into the unity of faith. But this incident remains proof that God can be heard even in circumstances where the possibility of faith is excluded. It is, then, a break-

through into the sphere of the pagan, into that of
nonbelief, which—contrary to usual assumptions—
does not, as such, imply a conversion to faith. Rather,
there is an objective ability to accept a reality that is
recognized as a reality; and while that is not powerful
enough, for Balaam, to transport him to faith, it is
powerful enough to stamp him as a prophet. The essential element in his mission is that he "see(s) . . . ,
but not now", "behold(s) . . . , but not nigh"—
phrases not merely suggesting the presence of the
sign to him but also defining his standpoint. A believer's beholding would be "nigh", even if not
"now". Balaam sees within the objectivity of his vision, but from a distance that is imposed on the non-
believer because grace does not touch him in such a
way as to make him a believer. In all that he does by
virtue of the supernatural quality of what is given to
him, he is a mission-bearer, one who stands out from
the crowd, who has been taken up into a temporary
state of obedience. And in this element of the "not
now" and "not nigh", a provisional exclusion is inherent, which nevertheless also contains a promise:
his hour, too, will come. He, too, will one day come
to experience the here and now. And his obedience
vouches for some purpose that God holds ready for
him.

   His prophethood is associated with a limited task,
and his effect will also be a limited one. But it will help
to allow other missions to be perceived more clearly

and also to make more evident the diversity of the ways of God, who is able to bring forth not only a Paul out of Saul but also, for a time, a messenger out of a heathen who remains a heathen.

GIDEON

If the missions of the Old Covenant are conferred in order to bring God nearer to men, to convince them of his greatness, to demonstrate his way of putting man to use as a helper, then Gideon's case can be shown to involve a two-sided mission. It is his part to test God, and it is God's part to test him. The first means that Gideon needs to appropriate his mission himself, by independently confirming it, in order to achieve full certainty that he has, indeed, been sent. In his approach to God, he is permitted to specify various conditions. God never tires of allowing himself to be tested by him; God is dealing here with a timorous man, whose fright he does not simply dispel but whom he allows to serve him in fear and anxiety. Gideon is permitted to appear before God with an attitude of near scrupulosity. When the angel comes to Mary, she says Yes; and in her Yes she manifests the sureness, the lastingness, and the directness of her mission. Everything is determined once and for all; from that one standpoint her entire mission can be surveyed; it persists, it develops, in unflinching loyalty and fearlessness. When the angel appears to Gideon, he is uncertain; he is partly inclined to believe, cannot assure himself that this is correct, and begins his questioning. He questions because he has views of his own (Mary has none). "Alas, O Lord GOD! For now I have seen the angel of the LORD face to face"—which makes him think that he is about to die. He constantly draws on all his powers of human reason to come up with tests that might help him gain certainty. He moves ahead step by step, in a state of anxiety, of human want and indecision. He was a pious man when the angel came to him; he wanted, after all, to serve his people, and in so doing to serve his religion and hence God. But he had opinions about that service, an awareness of his own nature and limitations, of his talents; he knew himself and, somewhere along with that, also knew God. And thus he cannot believe that he, *being what he is*, could really be a mission-bearer. He does not immediately allow himself to be used and tested by God but starts constructing a whole system of safety measures, not so much, at bottom, in order to make himself secure as to tie God down. Not so much in order to rescue himself as to rescue the commission in all its rightness and uniqueness. And his testing does, in the end, lead to his achieving security. Once he has gained possession of spiritual security, God initially presents him with human security as well, by placing at his disposal a superior military force.

For his part, Gideon can now live with a sense of security; he sees how the danger has lessened; how, when viewed and assessed in human terms, his undertaking appears quite feasible. But at that very moment, God starts testing him. He reduces the available forces. The commission is not intended to embrace some

unnamed number of helpers but is aimed precisely at
Gideon. He and no one else must confront a superior
enemy force. God wishes to show him who God is.
Step by step, he cuts back the numbers. And the many
who depart from Gideon are now like qualities that a
mission-bearer might have: his personal habits, his
spiritual wealth, his possessions—all those things without which one cannot get along in life. God keeps
cutting back, until Gideon reaches the point of nakedness of spirit, of utter renunciation, of pure devotion.
By discarding everything else, Gideon is divested, and
becomes more and more so, while the nature of his
task remains the same: to show complete obedience, to
make the impossible possible. God uses Gideon to
demonstrate, under the Old Covenant, what he will
demand under the New Covenant from those com-
mitted to following the Son. Surrounded by the great
masses, Gideon resembles the wealthy youth who
would like to do more but is astonished when told that
this "more" expresses itself through a renunciation that
was preindicated for him by God himself. Gideon was
alone when the angel spoke to him, and his backing
will be quite sparse when he moves against the enemy;
he must have a feeling of being unable to succeed yet
at the same time a growing knowledge of the reality of
God's superior might—of God's momentous potential
for imparting the supernatural to men, in an utterly
incalculable way, so that they can draw on God's power
to accomplish that which he expects. And when Israel
is saved by an obvious miracle, and the enemy's blood

is being spilled by its own hand, and Gideon is once again able to test God—although he now no longer wishes to test him—he shows his greatness by rejecting the prospect of ruling over Israel. God should be the ruler. Just how fully he belongs to God is revealed here. In his asking for gold from the spoil, however, and in the ensuing idolatry among the people, something again emerges of the human quality affecting him when he thought it necessary to test God and was counting on the greatest possible amount of human aid in carrying out God's commission.

Nonetheless, he remains unsullied in the context of his mission, because God has put him through so much and used him to exemplify various things—above all this: that God is always ready to let himself be tested but will not spare the tester from being tested himself; that he always links each mission-bearer to an absolutely personal mode of obedience, in order that he may fight for God as a true individual and that the divine intentions underlying his mission will show themselves most purely; and that everything must occur to God's greater glory. If Gideon had gone into battle with large forces, it would have been his human cunning, his forethought, his organizational talent that were glorified rather than the sheer superior might of God and his unlimited power to act effectively even through a hesitant man.

SAMSON

He has a mission that serves primarily to illustrate the gravity and force of vows. It is intrinsically oriented toward the coming mission of the Lord: for the angel appears to Samson's mother, too, and reveals her chosenness for this birth while linking it, similarly, to certain conditions that must be fulfilled. His parents, then, are also involved; they are to help oversee their son's mission and, in some degree, even to make it possible, since they create the accompanying conditions for the mission and are intent on maintaining them. In order for their part to be realized, they must give their assent while also grasping the magnitude of their responsibility. Further, it is not sufficient—since they cannot be equated with the Mother of God, nor can Samson be equated with the Lord—that the angel appear only once. Mary could, of herself, give one eternally valid word of affirmation. Here, however, Samson will need to give the assent pertaining directly to his mission; his parents have only to secure the conditions required for that mission to emerge. Since the matter is unclear to them, they question the angel twice and also have to discuss it with each other—as opposed to Mary, who keeps her secret to herself. Still, this linking of the parents to the son's mission not only presents a parallel to the miraculous birth of Christ but discloses an even more far-reaching intention on the part of God: the parents are to provide a suitable sphere in which their child's votive mission can develop. In a sense, Samson will take up his parents' vow and make it his own even before he reaches the stage of reason, and, in fact, from his birth onward.

The purpose behind his vow is to serve the greater glory of God; the taking of vows is a form of service supported by God. However, God does not merely indicate that he requires this form of service: he also equips it with a special consecration and strength. He endows Samson with supernatural powers that manifest themselves as physical might yet remain dependent, as such, upon a complete upholding of his vow. Samson thus provides a concretely perceptible example of the spiritual power that God is willing to bestow on the vows of his servants and of the fact that this power serves to glorify God. A whole cyclical dynamics affecting the force of vows is evident in Samson's life, interlinked with the parental sphere and issuing from conditions set by God. The long hair is a symbol of faithfulness; in its growing toward God, nothing of it is cut through and separated off, so that its force is fully evident. The short hair represents the breaking of the vow; it was not Samson who broke the vow by cutting his hair but, rather, the woman. And yet the blame lies with Samson, who had done wrong. The blame that cripples the maker of the vow can stem from himself or from something around him; but in either case it weakens his power. Samson, having taken

up with harlots, becomes a betrayer. But then he re-
pents of this, and God accepts his contrition. And
once again there is a prefiguring of things Christian:
repentance desires absolution and also receives it. And
so Samson is given back the power that points beyond
him to God.

His vow is marked by that human weakness which
makes its presence felt everywhere despite the strength
of God. For Samson's power is not his own but always
the power of God, the power of his vow and its upholding, in fact, the power of faith, which renders
faith receptive to the will of God no matter what form
that may take.

JEPHTHAH

Two things are to be observed about this mission. The first is Jephthah's change of social position within the family: the contemptuous early rejection, which he accepts in humility and faith, and the later appeal to return, likewise accepted in humility even if tied to conditions that he imposes out of an awareness of his mission. This first aspect is symbolic of the change in status, downward as well as upward, that God can ordain for his adherents when this serves his purposes and matches his intentions—a change, however, that in no way affects the mission-bearer's vocation. External positions of wholly opposed kinds can constitute the outer framework of one mission for purposes of humbling the favored and consoling the disadvantaged.

The second thing to be observed is Jephthah's oath, which is made in complete faith. And which is right because it occurs under the Old Covenant, when God was disposed to permit such vows. The conditions he set for men then were different; his justice could be satisfied through the upholding of such vows and even through their making. No matter how difficult they may be to uphold, they are safeguarded by God, so that their difficulty finds a counterweight in the beauty of being allowed to say Yes to God, in a Yes that persists beyond time and circumstance, and these two aspects are kept in equal balance. God himself makes the difficult possible and grants the recompense, which lies in the keeping of one's word, the increase in faith, the divine contentment. And this oath—whose nature is not far from the Christian vow of poverty, chastity, and obedience—is upheld not just by Jephthah alone but also by his daughter. The shared faith at the family's core proves sustaining. It sustains both Jephthah's sacrifice and his daughter's consenting sacrifice. When she wishes to bewail her virginity and her father allows her to do so, that takes place within her own mission, which is contained in that of her father.

The supplementary counterpart to this is the sacrifice by Samson's parents, who make their sacrifice for him before he is there; or more generally, the sacrifice by the parents of priests and members of religious orders, who offer their children to God in a way consistent with their times. God had drawn a veil over Jephthah's eyes; Jephthah did not know who would be first to come forth to meet him upon his arrival home; he is aghast when he sees that it is his daughter. In a similar way, parents might offer one of their children for the priesthood yet still be aghast when the choice falls precisely upon the one they love most; and yet be consoled again if that child, of his own accord, endorses the preexisting decisions or intentions of the parents and goes on to realize them. When God allows precisely the person Jephthah loves most, his daughter, to step forth from the house, he thereby shows the loftiness of his expectations regarding the sacrifices that the faithful are allowed to make. But also the greatness of his own preparedness to make sacrifices—for, not letting himself be surpassed, he sacrifices his own Son. It does not detract from the force of Jephthah's oath that he made it ignorantly and perhaps overhastily, for God heard it mercifully and looked after its fulfillment himself, granting what was most precious, then taking it back, and thereby revealing a meaning for later generations. He had shown that if, for the purpose of honoring God and fulfilling his mission, a man promises something without thinking it through fully, then God will help to ensure that the promise is upheld; and he had demonstrated—in everything else that happened, in the battles and other events in Jephthah's life—that he had kept faith with him, just as the maker of the vow had kept faith in turn.

SAMUEL

The essence of this mission lies in its aspect of continual confirmation by God, by events, by the people. The essential thing is not simply that Samuel remains pure, lives in obedience, and seeks counsel from God about the things he has to do; but, rather, that what he has done, what he is, what he represents and—in the eyes of God—had to represent through his mission receives the confirmation of the people in general. The people do not merely see him as a good man but constantly sense the nearness of God in and through him, run up against the mysterious in him, and thus experience it themselves. Samuel is, then, a mediator. He is that, not because of his own nature, but because he has a mission from God that is already implicit in his mother's petition: she wants to conceive him only if he is to be dedicated to God, to see God always before him. God complies with her request by taking her promise seriously, indeed, by having ultimately exacted the promise from her in order to be able to present her with this son. The situation here is not, then, like that of the Mother of the Lord, who is approached by the angel and told of what is to happen to her and what will require her assent. Samuel's mother must give her assent in advance, must herself pronounce—in her later years when she is already

49

regarded as barren—the Yes of fruitfulness and also at-
tach such conditions to it as will allow both her son's
mission and her own fore-mission to be recognized.
She is one of those female figures situated within the
spiritual environment of Christ who serve to herald
his coming, and it is not just coincidental that precisely
her son will anoint David to his kingship.

Additionally, it is part of Samuel's mission to show
how the natural and the supernatural, reason and obedience, human insight and prayer are related to one
another. He is obliged to do what he does not want to
do, to follow paths that are disagreeable to him and
that, in terms of his faith and religious understanding,
are not good paths. In the matter of choosing a king,
he has to do what pleases the people, although he sees
this as disobedience and has to have that disobedience
subsequently explained to him by God. Because the
people have estranged themselves from God, God
consents to their choosing a king but will turn that bad
development to good purpose—all of which illumines
with particular clarity the nature of the prophet's mission, since he has a gift for bringing God and his
people closer together. And in everything that happens, one constantly finds Samuel holding some decided viewpoint, not wrong in itself, yet having, in
each case, to obey and to change. God does not accept
the things that Samuel does right but, rather, integrates
them into something still better, allows the natural to
be overcome by the supernatural, reason by faith, insight by obedience.

Samuel knows that he is a mission-bearer who has been called three times by God. Three times at the ark of the covenant, the place where the signs of God's sovereignty are most visible. Again and again, the voice has aroused him from his sleep. The high priest misunderstands it—which clearly stresses the element of having heard but not recognizing—and by means of this process Samuel is better initiated into his mission than if things had gone totally smoothly. God does not make use of him as a prophet whom he nourishes through manna or the sending of ravens but employs him as a wrestler, a gladiator, who fights, not for himself and his mission, but for the will of God and its fulfillment. He must continually learn to say "not my will but thine". It is a kind of Ignatian breaking of his own well-founded will for the sake of the greater glory of God, who then, however, not only shows him his wisdom and acquaints him with his divine intentions but also lets him experience the fact that he is acknowledged by the people, that they become the fruit of his prophecy, that God is satisfied with him, and that he has fulfilled the position reserved for him by God within the kingdom of his missions.

SAUL

This mission is initially contained within the preceding one, since God inspires Samuel to see Saul as the divinely appointed king. But Samuel's mission is meant to become, later on, distinct from Saul's mission—as a mother from her daughter, one generation from the next, or a fulfilled task from a new one. And this fails to occur because Saul is incapable of dispensing with himself. The introductory stage goes quite nicely. He is recognized in God and is given signs intended to increase his obedience and faith, the fulfillment of which should, in his eyes, permanently confirm his already-effected anointing to the kingship, thus insuring that he has received the capacity to accomplish, before God, the divinely willed task. The signs involved are not merely certain more or less trivial ones; there is the sign of the triune God, linked to lamb, bread, and wine—a pre-Christian sign, one already structured in such a way as to imply that the bread is food given to him by God and that he should interpret this sign as implying not merely the confirmation of his office but an accompaniment, a nourishment, a daily strengthening, an aid to growing into the demands of that office. With the second sign, he undergoes a complete transformation of himself; his self-composure and his understanding, which had pre-

viously accompanied his actions and overseen their
execution, are to be taken from him in a way designed
to make him feel this transformation—to render him
suddenly full of the Spirit, a prophet among prophets.
And this is noticed by those around him as well, who
attempt to discover the explanation for his new nature
by asking: "What has come over the son of Kish?"
These things have been imposed on him as signs by
God, and they are strong enough to effect his complete
conversion and allow him to bear the office of king.

This is followed by a test of his obedience, a brief
prolongation of which is meant to teach him that
there is always something of a "surcharge" involved in
obedience, that one must always weave a strand of
personal merit into each instance of grace. Here he
falls short. He would possibly have been able to acquire the merit if the grace had not caught him so
unawares that his understanding was no longer able to
keep pace. He begins to act autonomously when
strictest obedience is required. He starts remonstrat-
ing with God about the test to which he is being put.
He senses the concrete, earthly stresses, but not the
supernatural assistance, his being held by God above
the course of events. And so he proves inadequate.
Although he has received the grace of kingship in
superabundance, he proves inadequate. He fails again
and again. He gained his mission through Samuel's
mediation; he was overcome by God's power; yet in
the context of all this he keeps seeking himself instead
of offering himself. He seeks understanding, not the

supernatural; comprehension, not belief. Thus one
failure follows another, right up to the time of his
death. He perceives his weakness and struggles against
it. But he does so with a kind of malice and bit-
terness; he tries to locate the shortcoming in others,
becomes envy-ridden and insufferable, and God punishes him by sending him a melancholy spirit. God
makes his task, not easier, but even harder when he
fails. He manifests himself as the God of the "always
more", who begins to make excessive demands precisely when his demands are not fulfilled. To intensify
his conditions precisely when the element of the un-
conditional is missing.

This is a mission oriented toward the Son. In the
life of Christ, there are things that can be compared to
the tests imposed on Saul. Moreover, Saul can be seen
as related to David in the way that the Lord is related to
the disciples who survive him and take over his teach-
ings in order to preserve and propagate them. The
Lord rejoices in the fact that he has disciples and that
revelation will go on being transmitted by them. Saul,
by contrast, is envious; he would like to gather everything good together and retain it for himself, to be
himself a summit. To erect an ultimate monument to
himself and his greatness that would rise up within the
Old Covenant, something completely delineated that
would remain linked to his name. He would like to be
devoted to himself and not devoted to God; he can
find no satisfaction, no joy, in the tradition of missions
in which he participates through Samuel; he would

like to break the chain in order to be something not allotted to him—although something greater would have been his lot if he had found the courage to regard obedience as grace and belief as a reward. His drawing back is a flight toward himself; he fails to recognize the man God wants to make of him but recognizes another instead who is not contained in his mission. Were he to recognize the man contained in his mission, he would be greater than he is; but he has become smaller because he has created a distorted image of God for himself and made himself the reflector of a mission not founded in God. Thus his estrangement is inevitable. His mission is broken off. And yet, in what he believed and in what he achieved through that belief, he formulated a response to God that, however inadequate it still was, prepared the way for the emergence of his successor.

DAVID

This is a mission oriented toward the Lord, but one
that occupies a midway position: David is neither the
first Adam nor the second; he stands midway between
them so as to illumine both. He stands between the
world of sin and the world of faith, at the precise place
where the two meet. And the man he has to exemplify
stands midway between the shepherd who unsus-
pectingly grazes his flock and the all-powerful ruler
who must perform the highest acts of wisdom. Although he occupies this midway position, his own existence nevertheless has no midway point: he always
has too little or too much; but both these extremes are
at times permitted in order to disclose a human stan-
dard that has to measure itself by the measureless, by
the immeasurability of God. Two things are to be
shown by this: the greatness of God's power, of his
justice and mercifulness and grace; and the unworthiness of man. And midway between these, where there
can nonetheless be no midpoint, the state of man under grace: his falling out of grace, his being born again
into grace—because God suddenly pronounces his
word of promise that he will not forget his servant;
that, wherever his servant is forced to flee, he will follow with his grace; and that, whenever his servant for-
gets God for a moment (an allusion once again to

measure, as opposed to the eternity of God), he will fill in that gap.

This is no cruel playing at cat-and-mouse, although it is a process of play, but something more like a play of light and shadow, with God ceaselessly reillumining what man has darkened and man turning his dark sides toward God so that God might brighten them again. The impossible and the possible stand side by side, brutally and implacably, something perhaps nowhere more concretely illustrated than in this stripped-down boy who confronts Goliath. There, David must be man, nothing but man, naked, in poignant bareness, unshielded, helpless, vulnerable. Goliath is strong, enormously tall, powerful, and armed: a symbol of God and his might. And David outwits that might. He outwits not only Goliath; he overcomes not just him; he overcomes, at the same time, his God. He appears before God in all his nakedness and weakness, with the result that God, as it were, allows himself to be outwitted by him, lets himself be caught by him within his own words, to be overcome; precisely because David is so weak, so small, yet so quick-witted and does not shrink from facing him in battle—so that the confrontation between David and the giant also symbolizes the struggle for grace and its power and superiority.

As well, there are the numerous little falsehoods, the cunning, the attitude of always knowing better, the self-advantaging approach, all of which would make David seem a rather questionable figure were it not for grace and God's mercifulness, and were God's

intentions here not so uniquely and so clearly oriented toward the Redeemer that God can, in this
instance, virtually pardon everything, condone everything, tolerate everything—because he will still
emerge in the end as the victor, because he gives
David a kind of reward in advance, loving him more
than he deserves, conferring more faith upon him
than he can actually accommodate. David stands before God like a child before his mother, knowing
well that the mother will always forgive, that she remains a mother, and that her word of love possesses
a validity that time can never negate.

And among the many evil things that take place
around him, that others claim to do, out of respect or
calculated self-interest, for him or in his name, what
nevertheless keeps shining through is his faith, his
trust, and his seeking for God. And his songs are always
signs of the way that he exists before God; of the presence of God, which he does not forget; of his being in
God's hands. It is impossible for him not to do God's
will, although he sometimes might wish not to do it.
But he also cannot be completely true to it (as Christ
will be) when he does it; and again, he cannot ever fall
as deeply into sin as Adam did. For he, David, is positioned as if God had brought him forward, from
Adam, up through the whole course of history prior
to him, yet simultaneously backward, from Christ,
down through the course of history subsequent to
him, in order to create in him a kind of mirror image
in which the reflections of the first and second Adams

are merged—not because anything of great impor-
tance depended upon such an image, but because God
nevertheless makes use of this image he devised, this
mirrored convergence he arranged, to adumbrate a
new revelation of himself, of his possibilities, of his
truth to his word, of his abiding in the Word that will
be the Son.

SOLOMON

Solomon's mission is one of the Spirit; as such, it correlates with David's mission, which was oriented toward the Son. For God the Father, the missions he confers on David and Solomon are oriented toward the concept of the triune God. Solomon requests from God the very thing that God is most happy to give: the godly. Were it possible, under the New Covenant, for the Father to charge a mission-bearer with the task of wishing for some particular thing, then no possible wish could give the Father more joy than one for a Son-related grace. To be permitted, in one form or another, to follow in the footsteps of the Son. For this leaves the Father in the position of being able to grant precisely that which he most enjoys giving: the Spirit. Solomon's mission, like his father's before him, not only has its indeterminate counterpart in heaven but corresponds to a quite specific intention of the Father's regarding Christian doctrine. Both of them, father and son, have the task of praying, of singing, of recognizing the divine and transmitting it to later generations in a form that they themselves have given it. Through Solomon's sayings and songs, posterity is to gain an insight into how fully he was recognized by the Spirit, how often what he himself recognized was in the Spirit, how the Spirit passed through him and enabled him to comprehend things in a way far exceeding the understanding proper to the Old Covenant.

Solomon's mission, which consists in the fact that he is seized by the Spirit and discloses this Spirit to his people, to his friends and enemies, by simultaneously capturing him in words—that mission is rounded off through the building of the temple. What has been captured is then transferred beyond words into the finality of stone, so that the whole people is seized by a new fear of God, by respect and love; undergoes conversion in a new way; and is enabled to rejoice, through a tangible presence, in the splendor of God's Word, in the precision of his directives, in the beauty of his abode. These formations in word and stone are meant to lend God's Spirit a visibility for which the Spirit himself strives but which is grasped by Solomon and actualized in a universally valid way.

When he pleads for understanding and insight, he knows that God will fulfill his request. But in just what measure he does not know, and he must learn through his own experience that God's measure is one of superabundance. He receives what he wishes: and this accords with his capturing of the Spirit. But beyond that, he receives the Spirit's quality of being ever greater: and this accords with the astonishment that overcomes him when he sees the concrete expressions of his mind and his wisdom. This twofold image of the Spirit in him, namely, as a capturing and as an astonishment, accords with his whole mission. Moreover, in the words he utters, in the sayings and songs he composes, in the temple he erects, his spirit comes into contact with something supremely intimate, which overpowers him. The image of whatever he has grasped is always immediately surpassed by the image of what is no longer graspable; there is the encounter here of God with man, of the supernatural with the natural, and ultimately of the ever-greater God with Solomon's spirit, which wishes to grow greater through God.

And to a certain extent, what he undergoes in his spiritual life is reflected in the nature of his external life: in addition to everything else, God also confers upon him social power, riches, the grace of being popular, of being allowed to rule and to be understood by the people, of being allowed to sow seeds in the souls of his subjects: God's name, his wisdom, justice, and greatness. Then follows, in Solomon's old age, his apostasy. God sees it, God punishes it; but in view of his mercy, and in view of Solomon's obedience and his request for understanding (he might, after all, have made some other sort of request), the punishment is limited and transferred to his descendants. And this is also done for the sake of David. There is a mystery here that points ahead to the communion of saints, in which anyone can accumulate merit for another and all share responsibility for each other; it becomes manifest in David, and its fruit is allowed to be harvested by Solomon.

On the basis of David and Solomon, one could construct a kind of advance notion of what the heav-

enly Father will do in order to reveal himself to mankind in the Son. Certain aspects of the Cross are dis-
cernible: the bearing of sin by someone other than the
sinner; the father's renunciation; the redemption with
deferment of punishment for the sake of a kingly father. . . . These missions supplement each other,
round each other off, have their visible side for believers; but they also conceal things unsaid, inexplicable,
which will enter into the New Covenant's great mystery of love, into the mystery of eternity and heaven.
For no matter how much heaven may stretch toward
earth and be conferring, promising, and fulfilling of
itself, it always remains greater than anything that can
be understood from an earthly standpoint. Mysteries
of purity, of goodness, of perfection remain open,
which can always be sensed by us original sinners and
thankfully accepted but never fully comprehended.

ELIJAH

This is primarily a mission of the contemplative life, that is, one of constant openness to what God may say at any moment. God speaks, and Elijah must listen. And listen each time in the precise manner that God's word requires; apprehend in such a way as to enable God to recognize Elijah's openness. It is not the case with him, as with others, that God must first over-power him in order to achieve his ends; rather, Elijah's longing for obedience, for carrying out God's will, is so strong as to result in a constant attitude of readiness. This readiness is childlike; he also experiences in a childlike way how God looks after his needs: for instance, in the years when God directly provides him with sustenance while he is devoted to prayer. He sees that this praying confirms his existence before God, that he inhabits a world transcending the confines of the earthly, that his contact with God remains a direct one. The way in which he is nourished favors the activity of prayer. And if God does not simply keep him alive without any nourishment at all, then this is in order that he might not entirely lose contact with the world, might not have only God's being in eternity constantly before his eyes, but can also observe God's workings within transient time. And through this observing, it is intended that his prayer will grow stronger, his faith increase, and his whole contemplative life be marked by an attitude of readiness.

Later on, this childlike aspect grows more mature: he becomes acquainted with anxiety. Anxiety about God, anxiety about the response that one makes to God—which, for Elijah, still takes the form of anxiety about his own life, about the fate that awaits him. This anxiety is the sign of a man's level of maturity. It is an anxiety unknown to a child but one that befalls a man because his knowledge is greater and because knowledge carries within itself the core of responsibility. This anxiety, like prayer, is a part of Elijah's mission. Also belonging to it are all the blows of fate that strike him, the unprecedented power that is transferred to him, the sense of powerlessness he feels in himself, the being flung back and forth between his own unworthiness and the power—suggestive of utmost worthiness—that is bestowed on him. He is tossed in all directions, so as to be God's servant in going as well as coming and to bear witness to his Lord. He has to deal with the mighty of this world but also with the dead boy; these, too, are poles of his mission whose outer aspects symbolize something inner that God has implanted in them.

And then, at the time of the drought, comes the command to keep watch for the approaching rains. And when nothing happens, his continued adherence to the command. He himself can only pray, summon up all the power of prayer, which is necessary for effecting the miracle so that the Lord's word might prove true: that he, the servant, is authorized to end the drought. He must hazard everything, squander his last reserves of prayer, so that *his* Lord might prove true. "As the LORD the God of Israel lives", he says—but does so with a commitment to relevant action. He will do everything to ensure that the others might come to see that his God truly lives. And so it is regarding the miracle of the rain, the offering on Carmel, and the fulfillment of every word that the Lord entrusts to him. Through his prayer, through his attitude, through the miracles he performs—but also through the acts of penance he therefore takes upon himself—he is a witness to the truth of God. He cannot but understand mission, in a kind of archetypal sense, as witness. There is no mission that is not a bearing of witness, and insofar as all missions are this, they can be traced back to his; for perhaps in no other does it become so apparent that God confers his missions in order that his truth might have its witness-bearers.

ELISHA

His mission must be seen as a three-part one. And, as such, it has an implicit relationship to the divine Trinity. Initially, there is Elijah's knowledge of his successor, a knowledge in the Spirit, a form of mission in the Spirit. This first part appears to lie outside Elisha's sphere, namely, in the conversation between Elijah and God, at a time when Elisha is living subject to requirements and in a state of obedience, about which, for the time being, he knows nothing, that is, he is at a stage of being unconsciously at God's disposal. And yet he is already acting within a mission characterized by the fact that Elijah knows about it and that this knowledge has been given to him by God. It is actually a mission with no commissioned bearer, a service about which the agent has not been informed, a life of mission-bearing within the Spirit.

The second part is the period during which Elisha lives together with Elijah. Elisha would be comparable to a son who does his father's will, shares the father's perspective, experiences everything the father loves, strives to emulate him, lives in most intimate connection with him, so that the father sees in him the fulfillment of his own will. And the younger one does not want to leave the older. Every time he is encouraged to do so by the older, he resists, because it is his duty to remain with the older until his passing. Then comes that episode by the Jordan, which is reminiscent of the baptismal scene at the beginning of the Son's public life. The water is parted in front of them. This is still not baptism, but it is a miracle involving water.

From that point onward, the third part commences, which is comparable to the earthly mission of the Son, who takes leave of the Father in order to accomplish the Father's will on earth. And then there are the strange repetitions of things that Elijah has already done; in part, this occurs independently and, in part, because the words of the Spirit are repeated: it is a sign of the coming mission of the Son, who—in oneness with the Father, in obedience, in dependence, in prayer—does that which is the Father's. "No one comes to the Father but by me." The Son must embody the Father. Thus, to a certain degree, Elisha must reclaim, reenact, repeat the miracles of Elijah: so that God's unity might be made manifest on earth; so that, through Elisha, Elijah might become known; so that, in the God who directs him, the God who directed Elijah might become apparent.

Those are the broad outlines of his mission. Also apparent in it, though only in an allusive way, are the sacraments. There is the crossing of the Jordan. The allaying of need through a flow of oil. The anointment of Jehu, which points ahead to the anointment of the Son and was a task passed on from Elijah to Elisha. The increasing of the amount of food and then—perhaps as the crowning incident—the revival of the widow's son, which is carried out in such a way that the body of the dead is brought into contact, member by member, with the living body of the prophet. A miracle that prefigures the Eucharist. And at the end, even the dead bones of Elisha are able to restore another dead man to life. The fleshly body that had been devoted to obedience when alive retains its power of bestowing life because it was created with a view to another fleshly body that will stay alive beyond death, not for itself, but for the purpose of unsparing self-bestowal on mankind. Thus this miracle, too, is a prefiguration of the Eucharist.

Elisha's mission of working miracles, viewed in its oneness with that of Elijah, allows many mysteries of Christ's Incarnation to become more understandable, regarding not merely the course of Christ's fleshly life and his obedience to the Father but also his eucharistic presence, in which something that initially appeared purely human shows its divine origin and power. Occasionally, Elisha speaks the words "Hold your peace": for example, when the sons of the prophets attempt to question him about the vanishing of Elijah. For him, this vanishing of his master remains something like the night of the Cross: "My God, my God, why hast thou forsaken me?" And yet: "Hold your peace." Hold your peace, so that the word of the Son might later be audible. Hold your peace, because now is a time of silence, with a view to the coming time of the Word. Hold your peace, above all because the hour has not yet come, and that hour belongs to the Father. They

are to hold their peace in relation to the mystery of
Elijah, so as to become capable of experiencing the
divine mystery of the divine Father, who, at his hour,
will send the Word. It is a cautious knowing, a gradual
inauguration of the process, a sign of that which will
come *if* God's will is done, if Elisha really learns, ever
more deeply, both through and beyond Elijah, how to
do the divine will.

ISAIAH

If the emblem of the Son is the Cross, whose vertical beam links the earth with heaven and whose horizontal beam points out toward an embrace of the whole earth, so the emblem of Isaiah is the saw: a being sawed up and scattered in all directions, just as the different aspects of his mission point toward all regions and all lands. Isaiah leads a hard life; he is kept within a tie of close obedience to the Father, and this obedience reveals signs of the Son's coming life of obedience on earth. Each of his prophecies has its true explanation in the Son. Not, for instance, because the political events presupposed by them could be found to recur in the life of Christ, but because—in his knowledge of what is to come, of the judgment that will befall the peoples, of the holy remainder of his people—he is accompanied by a constant presentiment of Christ and possesses a prophetic certitude that, while not needing, under the Old Covenant, to be an essential part of his belief, is nevertheless an essential part of his hope. He lives in anticipation of the Son.

But even at times when his words are replete with the Son and he speaks in a less veiled way of the Son, he does so in an obedience that makes the coming consolations inaccessible to him. From a central core placed in him by God, he speaks out into a world, and amid events, for which he bears responsibility only via his role as prophet. His participation in salvation is thus one that comes about within a sphere over which he has no control. After every act of prophecy, he reverts, as it were, to himself, the Jew, without being allowed to experience the fruit of his prophecy or even its meaning as an enrichment of his life and prayer. He spreads threats, alarm, dejection, and anxiety throughout the world and also sows consolation and hope; yet he is not himself carried along in either direction: he is not influenced by his own proclamations, neither stricken by the warnings nor comforted by the consolations. He has to pray and live in his quiet room, as if he were not a prophet; and after every prophetic task that sends him forth and brings him public esteem, he ultimately returns poor and divested. His case is not like that of the prophets in the early stages of the New Covenant, who are so overflowing with what they have to proclaim that it coalesces with their faith and fills them with consolation. Isaiah experiences the hardness of the words he has to speak merely as a general hardness within his existence and does not make any connection between the two. This is already quite strongly a suffering that inherently subsists in the suffering of Christ yet apart from any realization of this. Even when he describes the suffering of the servant of God, there is something arid in his suffering, devoid of any connection with his prophecy, as if he never gains insight into the possibility that this might be a cosuffering. In his prayer, the hardness of the words strikes him as a unified totality that remains closed up within itself. Here, he is not unlike a poor man who has to deliver a sermon on poverty and speaks at length about the effects of being poor without basing this on his own experiences but on the subject itself, on the mere concept. Thus Isaiah participates in an experience that is of divine origin but without being permitted to alter the balance of his personal experience in any way.

When he makes political prophecies, he speaks on the basis of a detailed knowledge of things yet by no means after prior reflection. In the midst of the situation as known to him, he has to say things that do not stem from his experience, things for which he must assume responsibility only after he has proclaimed them. He has to be in agreement with them even though they are not expressions of anything he has accepted beforehand. His abiding acceptance lies solely in the fact that he keeps himself available to God as a spokesman or instrument, allows himself to be used for whatever God demands of him, in subjection to a hardness whose necessity he cannot fathom.

JEREMIAH

He occupies a midway position between God and man that is characterized, not by a state of equilibrium among all the things connected with his mission, but by a process of being tossed back and forth. It is a midway position, not in the sense of a dividing line, but in that of a swinging pendulum, which traverses a large area between God and man. Or again: he is positioned midway between the objectivity of God and the subjectivity of man and, indeed, in such a way as to be laden from the start with the qualities of objectivity, which must then be repeatedly cast off by his subjectivity. He had always possessed his mission, before he was born, before he was able to express an opinion about it, to say Yes or No; he had always been chosen for, and charged with, this mission. And when God presents him with the actual commission, he resists, in the opinion that he is not worthy, that things will not go well or might totally miscarry. He has no doubts about the truth of his prophecy's substance, insofar as he was able to receive what God was conveying to him. But he does not see himself as a potential transmitter of such words. And when he finally accepts his office, he has, to a certain extent, sided with God because of the necessity of his mission rather than from personal choice.

At every moment when he is actually engaged in prophecy or is otherwise carrying out his task, he possesses the sureness of one graced by God, a sureness, however, that deserts him once that task is over. He has to endure so much mistreatment by the people, who vehemently reject him, that God's objective viewpoint is lost to him, while—more or less as a result of the rebukes—he enters into the arguments of the people and has to grant them a certain reasonableness, indeed, even a necessity. He is repeatedly made a scapegoat by the people; yet he feels himself to be primarily the scapegoat of God, who treats him badly, who is in no way willing to adapt the scale of his mission to suit his human proportions. And he complains. He complains because he has to persevere in this impossible midway situation, because more objectivity is demanded of him than he finds bearable; he complains because his body is abused and his whole nature inclines him toward choosing a more comfortable kind of life. And yet so strongly is he disposed to take God as his master that new tasks can scarcely arise within his mission before he is on the way to carrying them out. Even when he takes an indignant stand against God, he knows that he has already lost, has already said Yes, because that Yes was spoken by God and not by him, a Yes that is stronger than his life. What he dreads most is the substance of his prophecies. He must always say precisely what he by no means wishes to say, something that is not appropriate to him and that prudence also suggests would be better left unsaid, since he knows it will set the people against him again.

His prayer is a noteworthy point, because there he defends himself against God and men in a way that effectively reverses the prayer of the Son: whereas the Son, who occupies the ultimate midway position between the Father and men, shares the vision of the Father and sees through men, Jeremiah tends to have the vision of the people and to see through God's intentions. His prayer runs something like this: "Thy will be done, but might mine nevertheless also be done for once." As if God did not have the insight that he, Jeremiah, possesses as a prophet and a man. As if God, because he has not come down to earth, were lacking in real knowledge of human needs, as if he had drawn up unworkable plans regarding men and cannot win them in that way. He also knows what adoration is, but he practices it with a certain caution and reserve instilled in him by the sad results of his experience as a prophet. And yet his will to do whatever God wills is evident in everything, although accompanied by a kind of insight that precludes full surrender to that will. He has to argue with God. This rebellion is permitted by God the Father, with a view to allowing the truly complete submission of the Son to stand out in all its splendor.

Jeremiah remains, despite the greatness of his prophecies, a man with narrow limits; in the context of what he transmits, he participates fully in the objective greatness of his mission but then goes on—as if in periods of rest during which he would like to recover from that greatness—to find that he has failed to make proper contact with the people, who react with outrage against him, plunging him into grave danger instead of granting him the rest he deserves. That he is continually rescued from such danger, nevertheless, serves him as a sign that God has heard him. Yet that brings him no rest; he knows that he will not find rest until God takes him back again to him. He is familiar with the quality of the "always more" in what God demands, but he fails to show the accepting attitude of the Son and his saints; rather, he exhibits the restlessness of one who needs more in order to bear the more that is asked of him: one who is, however, intrinsically capable, in many respects, of accepting the Christian faith and of learning, from the Son and his example, to bear whatever the Father requires of him. After every new instance of being rescued by God, it seems that his prayer must at last have assimilated what it means to submit to things; and yet he rejects this and cannot do so.

EZEKIEL

Ezekiel's mission is one oriented toward the Kingdom of God as understood in the Christian sense: also it is a preparatory mission oriented toward the apocalyptic mission of the "beloved disciple". Ezekiel is positioned before God the Father in such a way as to suggest that he has absolute knowledge that Christianity is coming, that the Son will appear. And above all: that someone after him will be transported by the Spirit. He is constantly thrust, in ever new ways, into his mission—seemingly without God's troubling himself much about how things might stand regarding the personal faith and personal willingness of the prophet; God always presupposes his word of assent and views it as the most certain factor in this mission. God deals with him in the way one would treat a child, showing him everything step by step, but never so much that Ezekiel could lapse into personal doubts and anxieties. And God always distinguishes quite clearly between what is to be done without any delay and what will appear after that has been done; so that if Ezekiel were to ask himself—at times other than those filled by the directives of the Spirit—whether he is on the right path, he would receive confirmation and security from what would happen afterward. He is supported by the word that is conveyed to him and by the success of that word. From both these sides, however, he is very strictly guided, as if in each case the success were standing surety for the word and keeping the prophet on a quite narrow path.

Ezekiel's mysticism is similar to that of Saint John's. He is transported in the Spirit; his ecstasies have at times the character of a fully physical translocation, an absence from the surroundings in which he has just been existing and a presence in far-removed ones. The same unambiguous quality attaches to what he beholds in heaven. He sees, not just something or other, but quite precise things. The whole symbolic realm he beholds is also extremely well defined, with very much (even if not everything) proving, in the end, to be just as true as the objectively perceived truth. And the different levels of what he beholds—the different worlds, regions, times, as well as the different roles he has to play in these—already give his life and his spirit, but also his obedience, something of the breadth of the Christian vision. But lacking to him are the Christian consolations. It is as if, despite his having a very comprehensive view of his mission, he has to keep breaking out with the cry: "Things just cannot go on like this!" The punishment is too hard, the justice too exacting, the failure too plain—and the degree of faith is fixed as so absolute that the Jewish concept of God does not suffice. It no longer suffices for the mission-bearer, and it suffices just as little for those to whom he must appeal. In the whole context of his distraction, his failure—which extends to the interpretation of the symbols and perhaps even to the choice of words that express those symbols—precisely that place is left empty which, in the Christian faith, will be filled by the everlasting presence of the Lord. The religious correlations, the doctrinal principles, are implicitly there and can be educed with a clarity and necessity that herald the certain coming of the Lord.

Were one to make a detailed comparison between the visions of Ezekiel and Daniel and the Apocalypse of John, one would be able to trace in this the expanding sphere of the Christian teaching: from modest early intimations, through necessary basic structures, to full unfolding. And looking backward from the standpoint of the Apocalypse, one could better understand the promise in view of the fulfillment. Could, in fact, see the Father better in the Son: the path to the Father through the Son, including the path from the Son back to the Father of the Old Covenant. Considered in human terms, Ezekiel suffers under a wholly excessive level of demand by God, which has its basis in the inscrutable "always more" of the Son and in the promise of eternal life that holds the reward for so much effort but which must be inexplicably difficult for him because the New Covenant exists first as a promise and eternal life does not appear to be promised to him, the prophet, personally. His prayer is nevertheless guided by God and, in fact, in such a way that the inherent consolations, if not concretely sensible, are still extremely effective. In his consoled state, Ezekiel is permitted to receive God's grace; and even if

he finds things difficult at moments of reception or
during his numerous transportations and visions, he is
nonetheless accompanied, in the intervening periods,
by a kind of confidence that God gathers from the
coming fulfillment of the Son and instills for him into
the promise.

DANIEL

Daniel's mission, like Ezekiel's, must also be compared with that of the seer John: there are both similarities and dissimilarities. John, in his introduction to heavenly vision, is accompanied by the Lord; what he learns with the Lord and what educates him for his office of love is an introduction that resembles, in the sphere of the New Testament, Daniel's personal formation through the law at the time of the promise. When the visions of the Apocalypse are given to John, the Lord has long been absent from earth: the seer is granted participatory experience of a fulfilled heaven in the Christian sense, which nonetheless corresponds, almost feature by feature, to the heaven of the promise in which Daniel is allowed to participate.

Daniel's education is an extremely strict and painful one, since he—without realizing the connections—must become acquainted with the sufferings of the Son. He is, in a way, a righteous man among sinners. There are moments when sin shows him a face not unlike the one turned toward Christ on the Cross: it signifies death. But since the full death and resurrection remain reserved for the Lord, Daniel is each time brought just to the brink of death, when he is then rescued in a miraculous way; and this rescuing is symbolic of the Resurrection. In the den of lions, he experiences the extremes of threat by the power of evil, as do his comrades in the burning fiery furnace; but he is rescued by a force that is closely related to the force through which the Father recovers the dead Son from the tomb. In many of his prophecies, it is as if Daniel were building stairs for the Lord, stairs of the promise, along which the Son will follow in his fulfillment, upon which he will set his feet, making use of the steps that Daniel has constructed under commission from the Father even though they have only limited apparent meaning within his own mission. He serves what is to come, he knows the power of the promise; but he does not know the degree to which the Lord will build on him, how extensively his prophecies will be fulfilled by the Lord. And when he interprets dreams and sees into the future, every confirming element underlines the authenticity of his mission. He himself has no doubts about it; it stems from God, and he feels himself so obligated to God that he adheres to the law with utmost exactness, in order to thank the Father for the trust that has been given him. On the other hand, he adheres to it in a concretely lived way, so as to confront the Jews visibly with the vitality of their religion and to show the pagans what a man looks like who lives within the law. He sustains the law throughout his age, within a tradition to which he feels completely obligated, and this tradition is inherently directed toward the one the Son will create. The Son acknowledges it, and that acknowledgement seals the continuity of both testaments.

Daniel's interpretations of dreams are stages preliminary to his visions; they constitute an introduction to mysticism. His ascetic endeavors, the trouble he takes in explaining the king's dreams, the success of his interpretation—these convince him that he has access to a world closed to others, and they also procure for him, without his being aware of it at the time, actual access to the world of visions. The interpreting of dreams is for him a schooling in mysticism. An essential element in this is the closeness to the mysticism of Saint John. On separate pathways—the one via his association with the Lord on earth, the other (together with Ezekiel) via Old Testament paths to the Lord, who is clearly prophesied here—they both move toward a similar mysticism. Similar visions having similar details and similar general meanings—indeed, mutually supplementing, completing, and intermerging meanings—are granted to them, with Daniel being called to see, in his vision, the New Covenant in the Old, and John, in his, the Old Covenant in the New; while both are called to bear witness to the strength of the cohesiveness of all revelation and ultimately to the unity of the triune God.

A comparison of the visions of these three seers would perhaps also allow the mutual redemptive activity of the three Divine Persons to become visible in a new way as well as the influence of the three Persons on the three seers; the mutually interpenetrative life of the three Persons in heaven as it appears in the visions of the three seers; and, finally, the role of the three seers as members of the one body, instruments of the one God, mission-bearers sent from the one eternity.

HOSEA

Hosea's mission is oriented toward the Lord in his coming Incarnation. *Verbum caro factum est.* The Eternal Truth, which dwells forever with the Father as his Son, is to take on fleshly form; God is to be transferred into this sinful world. And of course he has his Mother and his foster father as guardians, who are also aware of the divine secret. Nonetheless, he lives among us as a man among the many, with a body subject to the laws of materiality, exposed to the random events of everyday existence; as one who must grow up, must develop in wisdom and knowledge, must grow in the usual human sense, as children grow in order to become adults.

This mystery of the Incarnation must be revealed by Hosea through a symbolic parallel. Like the Mother of the Lord, he receives his mission from God; it has been formulated from all eternity and begins with a task relating to the body. God speaks to him and determines what is to happen with his body; he sends this body to sinful women (the women assume the role of sinners); Hosea has to become involved with them, just as the Son will become involved with sinners, has to live together with them, as will the Son with us, and do so in a way whose realistic detail must symbolize the mystery in the midst of the fleshly self-surrender. When he fathers children with harlots, these children are to represent the relationship of the Lord to his people. Their names have a programmatic significance that expresses something willed by the Lord, since the Lord himself determines those names. While the early children represent, even through their names, both the curse that the Lord must pronounce upon his people and the turning away of the people, it is granted to the later children to illustrate the Lord's grace: the *gratia gratis data*, the redemptive will, the intervention, the efficacy of the Lord's grace. Through this bodily deployment of the prophet, there is something within the Old Covenant that casts an enlivening light on the Lord's relation to sinners, on his abhorrence of sin, on his cleansing of the temple (when, with bodily force, he drives out the buyers and sellers), but at the same time on the grace of conversion, on the "always more" of his love: proof that he has the power, in fulfillment of the Father's will, not only to gain conversions by force but all at once, as if quite offhandedly, to bestow them. Hosea's role in this is comparable to the role of a human body that, in connection with speaking the Son's word, heightens its effect; this is also the case with the second wife Hosea buys for himself and does not visit for a long period, so as to symbolize the captivity of the people, which lasts for a limited time and ends with the dawning of grace.

And the prophecies go on being made; Hosea fulfills his mission in word and in spirit, just as the incarnate Son takes up the voice of the Old Testament prophets and allows them to go on resounding, allows the Spirit to continue blowing throughout the world, and ultimately—on the day of Pentecost—sends the Spirit down to his Church from heaven. Hosea knows, however, the difference between body and spirit, since he does not undertake anything independently, at the behest of a spirit tied to his body, but always acts only in obedience to his Lord. In this, too, he reflects the Son, who does the Father's will. His life is like a premonition and, in some respects, a kind of anatomical sketch of the Son's earthly existence: what is present as a living unity in the Son is broken up into discrete elements in the prophet. The Lord God commands; the Spirit confers the prophecies and elucidates their meaning; and the prophet has to symbolize the Son's body—but in distinction from the Son's voice, from the divine will, because the Son will be the first to represent, in his divine–human existence, both the Father's unity of flesh and will and the Spirit's blowing.

JOEL

This is a mission oriented toward judgment and is situated as such both between the Old and the New Covenants and between God's anger and his grace. It is "between" these, not in the sense of a balanced halfway point, but in that of both the one and the other. Thus it is plainly shown in Joel's prophecies that there is nothing half-hearted about God: he curses or he blesses; he punishes or he rewards. There is his anger; there is his infinite love. The anger is a genuinely Old Testament one, which simultaneously signifies apocalyptic justice and is therefore a mirror image of both what has been and what is to come: of both the heavenly God of the Old Covenant and the heavenly God of the Johannine vision. And if the two images resemble each other, that is because John has to take over something from Joel, something that was there from all eternity; which means that Joel has vistas to disclose on the New Covenant: perspectives on God's anger that never pass away. And this also applies to the blessings. Words of the Old Covenant are mirrored in words of the New Covenant, words of anger and of blessing—so that it might be shown once again that the triune God is one, that the faith is one, that the Son does not destroy and pass over the Old Covenant but, rather, erects the New Covenant on its basis—that which is

coming on that which has been. When the Son himself, or his apostles, utters words in the Spirit, then
those can be words that have already once been ut-
tered, words with which the prophets have been inspired in the same Holy Spirit, so that the solidly
coherent structure of revelation is made apparent.

Some prophecies pertain wholly to the judgment
of sinners. These sinners are, in a way, anonymous, but
their punishment is not anonymous: it sees the individual wrenched out of his namelessness in order to
incur that which God's anger has deemed fit for him.
And the angry words of judgment, all the vigor that
resounds in them, Joel's obedience in unleashing the
most terrifying threats without mitigation, are meant
to show that those facing judgment will stand before
no fainthearted judge, that God's strength in judgment
has been prophesied from time immemorial. The full
strength of that judgment will be revealed at the time
of the Son's Cross, who will bear all the suffering all
the way to death, a form of justice that truly presupposes no weak judge. It is the countenance of the same
God that looks out from Joel's prophecies and the
Son's Cross. When words of Joel are repeated within
the New Covenant, this occurs in close connection
with the Cross: before or soon after it, at a time when
grace is diffusing a new light, which, however, is not
capable (little though that would have corresponded to
the Son's will) of mitigating the Father's justice in any
respect. But since Joel lives at the time of the promise,
the aspect of grace is largely concealed. Joel has to

prophesy through a kind of accession to the terrible, and that terribleness possesses for him its full reality. The sense of terror was lessened for his hearers only inasmuch as there was also prophecy of the descent of the Spirit and the salvation of the people, since the prospect of the Cross was counterbalanced by an anticipation of Pentecost. In the end, so much weight is attached by the priests to fasting, grieving, earnestly heeding events, that man comprehends that there is such a thing as merit, which confers on faith the possibility of suffering in advance from the frightfulness of punishment in such a way that the paths of grace will be more readily disclosed.

AMOS

Amos, the man, inhabits a sphere that is fully comprehensible to him: he has a piece of land, a family, an occupation. What constitutes that sphere is, for him, his world. Then: it becomes necessary for him to undergo the experience of poverty, and, in fact, in two stages. He has to be made homeless, be called away from his flock, be driven forth, and thenceforth exist in a state of uncertainty, in expectation of what is coming, in recollection of what has been; until the day when the Lord's voice makes itself heard again and consigns him to a much more severe state of poverty, in which he will no longer be allowed to stand by his own people, but must condemn them by proclaiming their evil deeds, and will finally die in a foreign land.

He must take this poverty upon himself out of obedience; his receptivity to his prophecy and the experience of its realization are consequences of the first stage of obedience that he took upon himself when he left his flock. And then he is given the great visions that stem, for him, wholly from the realm of God; that have the character of the eternal; that introduce him to a realm not of this world, one to which he has no other mode of access than that of obedience: he must receive, actualize, and transmit what comes to him from there. He is an instrument in the hands of God, an instrument consigned to poverty by its very function. And when he perceives injustice in the people, the oppositions between rich and poor, and all the wicked things that take place in the name of money, then his own personal fate helps him to understand this properly. God has taken everything away from him; he has to experience what it means to be divested of everything; also, he cannot feel that these actions by God are a judgment, since God has blocked in him any sense of having been punished so that his sensitivity to the injustices done to the poor might be all the sharper. He is an instrument, a bare instrument, which God uses for the purpose of giving account of himself, an instrument not allowed to understand itself so that it might better serve what is not itself. God handles him less than gently; he is not permitted to have any sense of being loved, while it is through him—but also through God's words—that the love of others must be so much the more enkindled: especially of the poor. A love that is very clearsighted, since it discerns the evil in the wealthy, does not simply embrace every individual but makes distinctions, has to rise up against injustice among men, must be an effective and combative love.

The greatest aspect of his life is the fact that he went. That he allowed himself to be driven out of his rightful hereditary position as a herdsman and dresser of sycamore trees. It was his personal folly to have obeyed God so blindly—a folly that is at first by no means rewarded but brings him the bitterest of consequences. And his prayer would necessarily have been as bitter as the lamentations of Job or Jeremiah had he not also been given such an overabundance of love for the victims of injustice that he loves God reverently despite his personal fate, far above and beyond what God has done to him. His love, his sense of justice, and everything he sees and mediates always remain completely objective, because he is willing to suffer in a context of dependence on God that is constantly suffused with the same vigor as his initial renunciation. He does not grow half-hearted, he never wearies; even when things are difficult, he maintains a fully vital presence before his God.

OBADIAH

One could regard the missions of all the prophets as measures undertaken by the Father in order to mark out the place of his Son. He concedes this and he claims that, he sketches and he erases, he paces things off, he erects barriers, he closes in and he opens up. He brings the missions into play as a means of generating activity that will facilitate things for the Son. Facilitation with a view, not to the Son's person, but to his message, to the Christian teaching: its foundations are laid, the underpinnings for the Son's word are constructed. And in a different way through each prophet. One must voice laments from the depths of his heart and allude to a Cross he does not know, yet still foresees. Others must merely utter words that will be taken up as prophecies and fulfilled by the Son. For one, what is involved is a highly personal task, with the result that the man himself merges into his mission and it is necessary to examine him in order to understand the mission. With others, nothing is important except what they say in God's name; after that, it is as if they themselves pass into retirement; indeed, they do not need to leave behind any sign at all of their ever having existed apart from the Lord's word. It is to this latter group that Obadiah belongs.

In his prophecies about judgment, he identifies all

that Edom had failed to do and how that was at odds with the Lord's intentions. He gives a justification for judgment. He reveals to the Edomites the sins they will have to confess. Generally, it is a lack of love that has shown itself in the most varying concrete forms. All this is a preparation for the Lord's commandment to love one's neighbor; since the Edomites in no way fulfill that still unspoken command, judgment and sentencing are sure to come. That it will be carried out is something as nonhypothetical as their sins; it has its historical dimension just as do their sins; there are judgments by God that are to a certain degree historically verifiable, so that those punished can discern in what happens the truth of what had been prophesied. They may not have been capable of grasping the whole meaning of the prophecy; but even those living later, at the time of the Lord, will not be capable of immediately grasping the fulfillment through the Lord. Similarly, what is initially evident in the prophecies of Obadiah is that aspect of their truth which is related to, and is bound up with, his own times; yet that aspect is true only in a secondary sense, since the full truth will first be evidenced in the Lord himself. The statements of Obadiah have their greatest truth in Christ; and it is through the negative realities of sin and judgment, as represented in the words of the prophet and stemming from divine inspiration, that those Christians who follow the Lord, who endeavor to adopt his teaching and to understand it, must learn to recognize that there is room for the positive realities of the commandment to love, of confession, and of absolution. Obadiah remains completely enclosed within the Old Covenant, yet he completely opens a path toward the mysteries of the redemption of the Son.

JONAH

This is, so to speak, a mission that operates against itself, inasmuch as it aims to preserve a place for man within the actions of God but ends by demonstrating through this the superior might of God. God calls; Jonah does not want to obey. On the basis of this initial situation, one escalation after another develops, each evidencing the power of the caller. He not only has a voice for calling but can draw, within his calling, upon whole systems of power before which all human cunning breaks down. The man seems to become smaller and smaller, and smallest of all in the presence of the continually intensifying call from God. God lets himself be measured against the man. He constantly allows the man to run free for a time, to start trying to realize some goal that is directed against God, to hatch some plot—but almost as soon as the man has begun with this, the call makes itself heard in a new way, and the man, unable to escape, becomes trapped in ever-increasing difficulties.

And yet, up to a point, the one being called is also always obedient. He manifests, to a certain extent, the freedom of obedience, since he becomes engaged in a conversation with God that is not a prayer but, rather, an attempt at self-justification—which is why it is not included within the mission of the Son, who makes a prayer of his every word to the Father, but takes place before that. On the other hand, God wishes these words of Jonah's to be expressed clearly, so that God's position on the matter might become evident. It is not a self-contained mission that is acted out here but more a missionary situation exhaustively depicted in all its facets, so that anyone subsequently called can use this case to test whether his refusal can hold firm and to what extent his acceptance will be enduring. Jonah's refusal may gain him a certain distance, but it allows him to be shattered on the unyielding will of God. On the other hand, his acceptance does not correspond to the plans he has constructed for himself. Everything depends on God, and nothing on man; everything on the one who calls, and nothing on the one called. Through Jonah's example, the mission-bearer is to learn that the obedient man, no less than the rebellious man, is always outstripped by God. That we can perhaps attempt to do the Father's will but that this will is so powerful as not only to annex our will but also to prohibit it from planning things on its own and demanding guarantees and concessions from God. Jonah's querulousness is the sign of an incorrectly understood obedience. He has been overpowered and has obeyed; he could have had things easier from the very start, but it was intended that he should be made to feel God's hand, to gain new knowledge of the one who calls, and to become aware of his own inadequacy in the very act of accepting. And when, in the end, God turns to the city and the task of realizing his merciful intentions toward it, ignoring Jonah and leaving him behind in an almost laughable situation, what remains for the prophet to derive from this example of God's mercy is precisely the sign that God wanted to give him: that he is greater than any mission and his will greater than any human concurrence. And that the essence of the matter is not what man says but what almighty God does.

MICAH

This is a wholly unified mission but one produced out of the prophet's knowledge and insight and out of what God asks him to do—a mission that draws together all that went before in order that it might flow into the Son's mission, which is already alive, already there, inasmuch as its voice reveals its presence. Throughout everything, the mercifulness of the Father becomes perceptible in the Son, with a kind of certainty that is not one of some future time but of the now, built upon what is of yesterday and the day before that. The people have sinned, the people are punished; at the center of the prophesying are quite indisputable things that are known to the people, words through which they recognize their misdeeds; the prophet's voice confesses on behalf of the people, recounts all their failings. Then the absolution from him who is to come: from the Son. Again and again the prophet returns to what once was, to what the fathers and forefathers of ancient times had known and done—to their blame, their chosenness, the innumerable signs of the activity of the living God, who not only took note of the people's homage and adoration as well as of their rejection and sin but always added his comments through acts of reward and punishment—so that the prophet's words effectively unfold a concise outline of the history of redemption, through which the truth of the words is to be made recognizable. The word of the past flows into the word of the future, God's current disposition into a heightened anger and an infinite mercifulness. Some of the words are, once again, apocalyptic: the vision of the woman in travail, who is simultaneously the city; the woman's pain, her humiliation, her being actually driven away, her having to submit to every sort of mockery and contempt—until the hour of mercy, of redemption, of the arrival of the Son. And inherent in all the prophet's historical words is a quite direct relevance, a visible presentation of the personal guilt: each one recognizes the reference as being not just to someone or other but to himself and his tribe and his entire people—to himself in the completely unhistorical uniqueness of the sinner who stands before God; and to his people in their historical context, yet no less personally for all that: the people as preexisting the individual sinner who hears the word, but still as codetermined, cocorrupted, plunged more deeply into guilt through him.

Here, God has conferred the gift of prophecy on one who knows, who recognizes, whose own capacities would have enabled him to speak many of the words he now speaks under commission. God expands this knowledge and insight and consciousness of guilt in order to make his own divine cognition, deliberation, and judgment accessible to Micah—so that the human word becomes a purely prophetic one and the implications of the then-existent situation are widened into the implications of the entire world's responsibleness before God. The word thereby takes on a certainty for the prophet, whose force leads him to the spontaneous insight that the estrangement of the people from God cannot continue in this way. Nevertheless, the image of God remains so much the Old Testament one, weighed down by so many threats, that the attempts to convert specific individuals always prove unsatisfactory, and each of those involved cannot but long for a new solution from God, a new act, a new covenant. And God cooperates in this longing, not simply inasmuch as he himself generates and excites it, but inasmuch as he imparts the certainty to the prophetic words: something different lies ahead. The hope here is grounded in faith, and the hope gives birth to love: the love that God the Father holds and shows by heralding something new, a love that, while implying that the cup of humiliation must be drained to the full, nevertheless promises that this will be followed by the time of his great mercifulness. And the prophet also responds to this: he believes the words he speaks, he takes hope from those words, and he feels within himself a newly resurgent love for his people on the basis of hope and faith. He knows that God alone is at work here.

NAHUM

In this mission, once again, a distinction is necessary: between the man as the bearer of his mission and the prophecy as the objective content of that mission. About the man we know nothing, although his contemporaries knew him, had formed an impression of him, and were acquainted with his views. For posterity, God lets him be wholly submerged by his prophecy; he has only to recount his terrifying vision and then to vanish, as a personality, beneath that. For he represents God's anger and does not need—as opposed to Elijah—to illustrate in himself both God's power and his own relation to it. God's power lies in the message. God's voice, this quite concrete voice, shows no concern about its hearer and its mediator, only about its message, which will be confirmed when what is foretold actually comes to pass, without Nahum's having to play any further role. Although images occur that are apocalyptic, he does not need to speak about himself, to say that he is a seer or relate what the angel tells him and the nature of his own attitude to that: recording, frightened, gladdened. He is objectified to the point of acquiring the isolation and finality of a bare prophetic voice. When God makes use of *a* man in order to issue a prophetic message, he does not necessarily have to use *this* man.

The second aspect is the content of the prophecy:
the destruction of the city. Here, emphasis is probably
placed most strongly on the weakness, the futility of
human resistance to God's will. It is still not the
weakness of the Cross, not the weakness of accession
to the will of the strong. It is a weakness *against* that
will. But also a weakness as punishment. The strength
of the city's inhabitants lay in their sins; they have de-
ployed their power, their guile, their intellects against
God and his commandments. In all of that, they were
conclusively proven too feeble. Their punishment is
not just the fact that their city is unceremoniously
razed to the ground but that they know about this
without being able to do anything to stop it; that they
are to experience, stage by stage, the truth of the
prophecy in all its horror and are overcome by a
weakness that precludes any effective defense. Varia-
tions on this weakness and futility are presented
through many kinds of images; the prophet brings in
everything men can devise in order to defend a city
and save their lives. But all is in vain. Powerlessness
stands against punishment, not the powerlessness of
acceding to God's will, not a personal incapacity that
participates in God's strength through obedience, but
weakness as such. Through disobedience, God's creature, to whom God had lent insight and strength, has
become useless. Man does not cease to devise ruses
that he thinks will protect him; but nothing works
any longer when only God's anger and prophecy still
hold valid.

The echoes of apocalyptic imagery are like a constant warning that the Old Testament, through its prophets, directs also to Christians: they must not forget that the images of heaven remain the same, because the Son does not displace the Father but, rather, effects his will. Because the Christian can experience things in the faith of the ancients that enrich his own faith. Because the prophets are also addressing him.

ZEPHANIAH

This mission begins by way of certain facts about Zephaniah's own being. He is not just someone or other; he has a family tree, he is widely known, his standing is established. But then he disappears completely beneath his prophesying, in which no regard is shown for his personal status. The mission asserts itself straight through him, as if his identity, although known to everyone, had been forgotten. There is something brutal about this, insofar as it thrusts him, together with his self-assurance, his personal sense of "here I stand", into the words he has to speak and whose significance is so great that he no longer comes to expression in them at all. What he expresses is the word, without being asked to take a position on it. The word is the absolute. Initially, as a word of anger. God reveals his whole power in anger. It does not worry him that he has created these men, that this is his world. He looks upon it solely with hostility. It has set itself against him; he will sweep it away. The threat has a clearly radical character, suited to terrifying the peoples and the individual sinners. And in the midst of this come words of conversion, seemingly quite out of context, since God will enter into no compromise, negotiate no bargain, but issues his warning from the standpoint of the absolute and as an absolute demand.

Then everything is cast in a new light once again when God reveals what he intends to save. It is Zephaniah's mission to find his way among all these absolute values—destruction or admonition or survival of the humble and lowly people—to the extent that he has to articulate them as the words of God for which he is a mediating voice. But nothing is ever said concerning how he himself feels about this, because it is not his part to feel anything about it. And here it seems to become understandable why God chose him, the eminent man with his family tree, to be the speaker of these words: precisely *because* he is somebody, and knows it, he is also capable of knowing that he has to be nobody in the context of this role. It is not a personal renunciation, accompanied by many deliberations and inner misgivings, but a total sacrificial commitment to prophetic service. And in order for future generations to see how radical that sacrifice was, the family tree is outlined at the outset. Zephaniah's disappearance into his mission is meant to fit into the pattern set by the absolute nature of God's demands, his absolute anger, and his absolute sparing. God subsumes his prophet, as a man, in the absoluteness of his word. This case is not like Jeremiah's, in which complaints are possible, in which the prophet is so strongly affected by events that he expresses his own opinions about them. It is something so total as to border on anonymity. But the God with whom the content of the prophecies originates is a God of endless possibilities; the peoples are to become familiar with the profuseness of his expressions of power in view of the coming revelation of the Son. They must learn to understand the nature of the sacrifice that the Son makes when he becomes man, the nature of the Father whom he leaves behind in heaven. Already now, under the Old Covenant, God's countenance must become, through his authoritative words, more sharply defined before the peoples: they need to know once and for all that their God cannot be confused with idols. They must learn again what form their image of him should take. All the words of anger are there in order to allow God's word to blaze forth in its omnipotence.

HABAKKUK

In contrast to Zephaniah's mission, Habakkuk's is a personal one: he is brought into a conversation with God and plays his own active part alongside the Lord's word. It is a conversation marked by an extensive degree of freedom and openness. The prophet appears less bound to any observable form of obedience that would also reduce his answers to aspects of that obedience; rather, he is meant to represent the freely believing creature in the presence of his free Creator. To be sure, he receives God's word in obedience and proclaims it obediently—yet that occurs in a context of utmost frankness toward God, even to the extent of daring to admonish God. This is not a reproof but an admonition that can be related to the Son's decision to become man. The Incarnation is intended to reveal God's triune love to the world, and Habakkuk admonishes God that he should finally show his mercy, should unveil his love—without knowing that God has long since decided to do precisely this. He cries out for this divine mercy; he needs it urgently for himself, for everyone, and also for the confirmation of his prophecy, for the time of judgment. In this conversation with God, Habakkuk is positioned midway between the Son and Adam.

And God shows him that the wicked rulers who are

against God have one main thing in common: imper-
manence. Evil has no stability before God. He gives
many examples of that which cannot endure. But suddenly he turns to the prophet with this command:
"Write the vision." So that it might be read. So that
what is permanently valid might be preserved. What is
permanently valid is the eternal Word. And the implicit reference in this act of writing is less to the act of
Moses, who writes down the law, than to the act of
John in the Apocalypse. By commanding Habakkuk
to write, God wants to ensure that his Word will endure throughout all time. The prophet's words, too,
including his admonition to God, are not to pass away.
And the prophet does as he is told and preserves the
permanently valid. God the Father sees that the man
Habakkuk has his everlastingness in Scripture just as he
will see that all men have their everlastingness in the
Son. The same divine act is repeated on different levels
so that God's power might become evident in its full
scope.

What has permanence because it is God's and what
lacks permanence because it is evil are the two poles
between which the entire history of Israel can be seen
to be played out. But the life of the Son can also be
better understood in those terms—the Son who refers
to the old prophecies; who makes the Word of God,
which he himself is, come true; who, through both his
coming and his continuance of directions from the
Old Covenant (where he is spoken about), lends the
Old Covenant not only a new meaning in him but also

a meaning that has always endured in the forever-enduring Father. The transient prophet, a man existing in transient times, thus participates, through his prophecies and through God's mercy, in the perduring of the Word of the Father. What is central to Habakkuk's mission is the way he is linked into the permanence of God, not merely as an instrument, but as a free agent whom God loves and who loves God.

HAGGAI

Haggai's mission is the taking over and handing on of a divine mystery that possesses its full validity in the Old Covenant and is invested with that validity in a new way under the New Covenant. It is the mystery of the temple but also the mystery of the Eucharist. In the temple, God has chosen for himself an abode that should be more important to men than their own homes; similarly, the eucharistic life should also be more important to them than their bodily lives. To be sure, the prophet receives his words here in a relatively straightforward form that can be understood in the context of the Old Covenant, one that the Jews will be able to grasp; everything is referred to by name and appears as a self-contained reality. As if God wanted nothing more than the earthly temple and were admonishing, encouraging, and consoling his people into building it. And that is undoubtedly the case; no matter what prophetic content the words may implicitly hold, their initial effect on the hearers is intended to be one that will make them conscious of their sluggishness, their resistance, their hesitation, along with the precise implications of the demand, its achievable nature, the means that would have to be employed. They can realistically measure the gap between their inaction and the action that is demanded. But beyond this there remains a mystery. The prophet knows—from his prayer and also because a shaking of the world is repeatedly mentioned in the words he receives—that a life must come from another world and will require an earthly house, and that we ourselves are to be that house. If it is still not possible for God to abide in the temple, then that is because men still fail to comprehend the urgent need for this dwelling and regard their own dwelling as more important. God, however, will shake the heavens and the sea and the earth in order to enable the coming of the Promised One. The arrival of the Son will herald a new form of God's abiding.

Thus the prophet from the Old Covenant must become the bearer of the good tidings in the period leading up to the New Covenant and must express the fact, through what he proclaims already in his own time, that the temple and the Eucharist are absolute demands of God the Father and the Son in their unity—a unity that transcends him and thus enables him to assert things about the arrival of the Son that are true yet far surpass all that he knows. His prophecies are also meant to influence the Lord's ancestors, so that the race might somehow be stirred, its chosenness become evident as well as its reward: being the signet ring of God! This reward has the character of the Son, because there is a clear relationship between the Son and the signet ring: insofar as what will go beyond the chosen one is the Son, who, however, circles back into the chosen again in order to abide in him—and thus a chain of chosenness and abiding already begins to be

formed. Silver and gold are mine, God says. He already
demands the best of materials for his house; he en-
courages the builders, teaches them to renounce things
for his sake, an external renunciation that amounts to a
training in poverty whose effect is on inner qualities—
so that, when the external world is shaken and the Son
arrives, the prophecy might be fulfilled, the way might
be opened for a new poverty in the form of obedience
(as a renunciation of one's own house), and the Lord,
who has been abiding in the temple, might take possession of men and prepare an abode for himself in the
man who loves him and whom he chooses.

ZECHARIAH

Zechariah's mission, more strongly still than Isaiah's, is one directed toward the New Covenant. Even if the apocalyptic visions are partly different from those of John, their redemptive significance makes them such as one would hardly expect to encounter in an Old Testament prophet. But he is the man who is permitted to speak so openly, so simply, and so naturally with the angel of the Lord that everything is made clear to him, the man of the Old Covenant, from the perspective of the New as well as in relation to something present. His task is one that entails a vision of heaven, a vision of the Holy Spirit and his activity, and a certain understanding of God's triune nature; and all this is for the sake of confession. Confession is elucidated to him through the example of the high priest Joshua [in Hebrew, "God is salvation"; also Jeshua: "savior"], and, in fact, not in relation to an acknowledging of sin, but with a view to the coming of the Son and his expunging of sin. The prophet sees the high priest not merely as being freed of his filthy garments and clothed with clean ones but as being immediately— through a total predominance of effusively pardoning grace—adorned, glorified, and made ready to serve in any way the Lord requires. This absolution is much more than a mere cancellation of guilt. It is also a mission directed toward confession, which now appears as instituted before the triune God, a mission directed toward the new institution of the sacraments, which are engraved in the one stone before the seven eyes. Seven sacraments before the seven eyes. Although it is a sanctification that is completely holy and takes place in God, man's participation in it is made clear by the prophet continually asking questions that are willingly answered. The questions signify merit, and the answers, grace. In order, however, that all this might not appear to be left hanging in midair, and relevant only to Zechariah, it is closely linked to further prophecies alluding to the life of the Son, who rides on the foal of an ass and whose side is pierced, giving rise to great mourning. The life of the Lord is depicted in such a way as to have undoubted reality for the prophet—certainly on the plane of vision and prophecy, but nonetheless as part of the seer's personal reality. For him, it is not a matter of having gained a theoretical insight into a content of revelation but of having experienced something. And when, in his visions, he sees many images that will be revealed again later to Saint John—such as the two olive trees that are the Lord's anointed—he sees them already within a confessional grace. He does not need to make confession; he *is made* confessed, that is, he receives the vision in a state of purity that enables him to see what God wants to show him.

In placing himself at God's disposal in this visionary role, Zechariah is like John. Personally, he remains within the Old Covenant, which, however, continues to be characterized by a potential to be expanded in obedience. He sees godlessness in a way that could also be the experience of a Christian; but he sees it in a symbolic form that has, as such, validity in heaven, so that he might understand that heaven remains continually open toward earth and that earthly things have a form of existence in heaven. The symbolic has its full effect: it speaks to him; he knows how to handle it, because the angel, who designates and interprets, gives him the key to this. And the city that is to be measured and become an open one, since it is overpopulated, and all the creatures he sees patrolling the earth and the angels and riders and everything that is part of heavenly plenitude—this is all aimed at giving the world a new meaning, a new unfolding and fullness, and the prophet's prayer a new strength, such as he knows will flow (for those to come) from confession, from purification, from being embellished in the Lord.

MALACHI

This is a mission that must distinguish between chosenness and nonchosenness and must begin by interpreting the mystery of chosenness in the framework of nonchosenness. Thus the priests are addressed first, then the nonpriests. The priests have been chosen for a role that implies their remaining faithful to the Lord. They are not permitted to depart from the letter of the law, are neither to take the Lord's words lightly nor to interpret them in their own way; they must adhere to all that their chosenness implies and be an example of the chosen to the people. Regardless of how any particular individual's chosenness has come about, it is something indissoluble, just as, later on, marriage will be presented to the people as something stable and they will be required to remain within contracted marriages. In both these contexts, the essential thing is permanence.

God's reprimanding words are presented, not as a one-sided address by the Lord, but in a dialogue, through which the arguments of the transgressors are brought into confrontation with the solely valid arguments of God. They defend themselves and put forward things aimed at emphasizing the difficulty of the task that God has set. But the word is cuttingly interposed to confute all this. There is the severity here of one who has chosen and does not want to be betrayed. The grace, reward, and consolation for those who serve God are not separately described, but only the hardness of the service; and the various reproaches suggest how difficult it can become for a man to remain in the state of chosenness, of priesthood, which is just as difficult as for a husband to remain faithful to his wife.

Then, however, the words of reproval for persons in these two kinds of position are linked to the promise of the coming, to the onset of fulfillment, in such a way as to reveal the intercession of the Lord, together with that of his servants and prophets, in its full efficacy. This intercession consists in enabling the sacrifice of the ones who truly serve to be accepted by God on behalf of the totality. The sacrifice and prayer of the coming Church are foreshadowed here, both in their strength and in their weakness. And the God to whom the sacrifice is dedicated is not only the strict Father who observes whatever is inadequate but also a helping God. There is no longer mere righteousness with a view to judgment; in many ways, one sees the nearing of grace. Strict though the words of reprimand may be, everything has a note of hope running through it that the prophet is allowed to convey to believers: that, because it is precisely *they* who hear his words, they, too, are destined for grace. Everything is described as if in a process of transition: judgment is at hand, but God himself positions his intercessors in front of it, his Son and the prophets, so that his anger cannot be fully discharged. In the final words, the whole of his love is already obviously present: they are words of the troubled Father, whose greatest concern is that his love no longer shines visibly forth; that his righteousness must take the form of punishment because those who are his—including even the priests—have broken his laws in every way; and that the people fail to return the faithfulness God has shown them. The distinction intrinsic to this mission thus alludes to the two basic sorts of social station within the Church, and the hardest that can be demanded is unveiled so that grace and forgiveness can find their ultimate place.

THE MOTHER OF THE LORD

When Mary encounters the angel it becomes clear to her—through what the angel says as well as through the ancient prophecies—that she must allow herself to be installed in a certain predetermined position. She knows about that virgin who will give birth to a son; she is acquainted with the passages in Scripture that foretell the coming of the Redeemer. She knows about all this in faith; the human knowledge that she possesses is expanded by faith into the fullness appropriate to a revelation. And now she must move into this reserved position in order to fill it herself: as accords with the promises of the Old Covenant, supported by the voice of the prophets and guided by the angel—who perfects her faith so that her word of affirmation, previously directed to the God of the Jews, now becomes a word of affirmation to the God of the Christians. The mission is thus one of the Old Covenant, and its task is that of moving herself, within the context of her spoken word of affirmation, into what has been announced by the prophets, so as to make it her own and to let it come about: to make, in the sense that Mary personally affirms her consent; to let come about, in the sense that her word of affirmation expresses her total submissiveness as the handmaid of the Lord.

The Messiah appears at the point of Mary's fulfillment of the mission of the Old Covenant. He appears as the New Covenant, and inasmuch as he is the
fruit of his mother's word of affirmation, he leads her
mission from the Old Covenant over into the New. As
the New Covenant, however, he brings all the promises of the Old Covenant to their fullness: in all of his
steps, all of his words, he shows consideration for what
is contained in the Old Covenant and what was decreed for his sake. At the point where Mary looks forward in order to let herself be fulfilled in the new, the
Son looks backward in order to fulfill the old. Their
missions do not, for that reason, run in contrary directions; in every respect they are firmly and closely inter-
locked, and there is nowhere the smallest margin for
any sort of error.

The loftiness of the Mother's mission lies in its being a mission in the Son. Every Christian mission is
contained in the mission of the Lord: it has its origin in
him. Mary, however, has to take herself to the place
from which the Son can come. In the context of the
divine plan, standing in that place means not only as-
senting, as a human, to being overshadowed by the
Spirit and giving, in faith, a word of affirmation for
which God himself is the guarantor; beyond that, in
the context of tradition, Scripture, or, in short, doctrine, it means accepting and holding a certain position so that, when the Son appears, this place, from
where he can begin his mission, might be occupied. A
place that is entirely one of promise, but that, since the

Son emerges from it, is fulfilled. One cannot say that the mission of the Mother ends at the point where the Son's mission begins, precisely because the Mother's mission, which commences under the Old Covenant, does not cease with the Old Covenant but continues to fulfillment in the New Covenant. Similarly, one cannot say that the Son first begins his mission at the point where hers is completed, because the promise is not a promise without its fulfillment. Human distinctions of this sort would be deleterious to divine grace. It is much more the case that the Mother's mission loses itself in, and is rounded off by, the Son's mission; while the mission of the Son, who wants to become a man among us, fulfills itself by merging with the Mother's mission. And he also simultaneously fulfills her, so that they both are able to manifest their completeness; and from that moment on, there exists an immutable state of being reciprocally bound together—the Mother to the Son and the Son to the Mother—which also provides the point of departure for all Christian missions.

In quite special measure, however, this is the point of departure for those dual missions in which two chosen persons supplement each other: through possessing either one mission in common or two missions that merge into each other. In such dual missions, there is a mystery of the imperceptibility of that point at which each merges with the other, and this mystery is the highest realization of that truth about being "two in one" in God. Anyone who wanted to try considering the Son's mission as one that extends, outwardly, into the world yet at the same time is rooted in an intra-divine relationship to the Father and the Spirit—since the Son is completely one with them in his willing—would run up against a similar phenomenon of each merging into the other, a similar mutual interpenetration that, as such, signifies fulfillment. The source of this interpenetration lies in the Son's generation through the Father and the Spirit's procession from the Father and Son, all within the perfect unity of their essential being; it also lies in the mystery of their eternal contemplation of, and devotion to, one another and their everlasting concord in everything that they will, do, and are.